PRAISE FOR *TO THE GORGE*

"This book is a beautiful tribute to the spiritual anatomy of the human heart, and the power of the wilderness to break us down and shape us into something far wilder and more tender. Every runner knows, or eventually learns, that running and grief can come together to reshape the dissonance of a broken heart into something like peace. Very few can put this experience into words. Halnon's story invites us to look at our own broken hearts, erode the walls between our protected self and our essence, and at the end of it all, jump up and cheer."

— Lauren Fleshman, *New York Times*
bestselling author of *Good for a Girl*

"*To the Gorge* is much more than a book about running. It will speak to anyone with a grieving soul and Halnon is a heartfelt guide for anyone on their own path to redemption and revitalization. Bold, courageous, and enthralling."

— Kathrine Switzer, author of *Marathon Woman*
and founder/director of 261 Fearless

"*To the Gorge* is both the story of a gripping physical feat, and also a deep reflection on the nature of grief and survival. We grieve because we love, and this is a book about how the power of love can nourish us through even the greatest challenges. A book you can't put down and one you never want to end."

— Claire Bidwell Smith, author of *Conscious Grieving*

"*To the Gorge* is so much more than a book about running, or even grief and loss. It's about how to live, and how to make your time in this world count and mean something. No book has ever made me cry more than this one—the kind of cathartic, full-body sobs that will leave you feeling inspired, grateful, and likely pondering how to create a legacy as powerful as Andrea Halnon's. A must-read for endurance athletes, aspiring endurance athletes, and anyone who is or has ever navigated a world-shattering loss of their own. This book will make you feel all of your biggest feelings, and invite you to think about how you want to live."

— Ali Feller, host of the *Ali on the Run Show* podcast

"This is nothing like that old notion *The Loneliness of the Long Distance Runner*—title of a popular novel from a lifetime ago. Emily Halnon's book recounts how a real-life, record-breaking long-distance run she undertook was made possible through the collaboration of a whole support crew of talented and dedicated fellow runners—good friends and family providing heroic encouragement in a way that is now common practice in the booming sport of ultrarunning. There's much to be learned from this gritty demonstration of how talented small groups can sometimes transform seemingly quixotic goals into life-changing accomplishments."

— **Ed Ayres, founding editor of *Running Times* magazine and former winner of the JFK 50-Mile**

"They say that pain is inevitable, but suffering is optional. Emily learns that lesson the hard way, when her mother is diagnosed with cancer. Then she learns it again, on her 460-mile run across Oregon in pursuit of a goal that is impossibly hard. But she confronts the pain. And transcends the suffering. As a result, her amazing badass mother, whose Northstar was 'possibility' and who embraces the motto 'stay brave,' lives on in her words forever."

— **Kenneth Posner, ultrarunner, peak-bagger, thru-hiker, and author of *Running the Long Path: A 350-Mile Journey of Discovery in New York's Hudson Valley***

"In this affecting debut memoir, athlete and essayist Halnon resolves to run across Oregon on the Pacific Crest Trail after her mother dies of cancer. While pulse-pounding descriptions of Halnon's athletic feats will be catnip for adrenaline junkies, what makes this sing is the author's remarkably clear-eyed approach to loss. Halnon's unflinching gaze elevates this above the crowded field of memoirs about losing a loved one."

—***Publishers Weekly***

TO THE GORGE

TO THE GORGE

RUNNING, GRIEF, RESILIENCE &
460 MILES ON THE PACIFIC CREST TRAIL

EMILY HALNON

PEGASUS BOOKS
NEW YORK LONDON

TO THE GORGE

Pegasus Books, Ltd.
148 West 37th Street, 13th Floor
New York, NY 10018

Copyright © 2024 by Emily Halnon

First Pegasus Books cloth edition May 2024

Interior design by Maria Fernandez

All maps by Ian Petersen—Map Your Adventure

Library of Congress Cataloging-in-Publication Data is available.

ISBN: 978-1-63936-665-1

10 9 8 7 6 5 4 3 2 1

Printed in the United States of America
Distributed by Simon & Schuster
www.pegasusbooks.com

For my mother, Andrea, who is every reason I'm a runner and who will always inspire me to live, write, and run with courage and joy.

CONTENTS

PACIFIC CREST TRAIL

OREGON
460 MILES

Prologue
LAST GASPS OF LOVE

They tell you that hearing is the last sense to dissipate, in the final hours of life.

"She should be able to hear everything you say," the nurse whispered to me, as I curled up in the beige armchair next to my mom's bed.

Her eyes were shut. A soft but decided seal of her eyelids. I hadn't seen them flutter open since I'd arrived in the middle of the night a few days ago, sprinting from the airport to her bedside after getting the call I knew was coming but never wanted to get. I'd like to believe that her gaze found me as I knelt beside her. I want to trust that the quiet crack of her eyes meant she knew I got there in time. But I'll never really know.

My mother had been moved to a hospice home after a rare and aggressive uterine cancer accelerated its merciless destruction of her health and body and life. She'd gone from diagnosis to hospice in a swift thirteen months. Her sickness had blindsided all of us—my mother was always

so healthy, so active, so on top of preventative measures like mammo-
grams, skin checks, and annual health visits. She'd called her doctor
on the very same day her first symptom appeared. But the cancer had
already advanced into its late stages by the time it whispered a hint of its
invasion of her body.

My mother, Andrea Halnon, was a running, walking, biking billboard
for physical fitness. She was one of the most active people I knew, and
not just for a sixty-five-year-old woman, but period. She was always out
pedaling around the countryside on her trusty blue bike, or running on
the web of dirt roads behind her house in rural Vermont, or traveling
around the country to race half marathons in new places like Glacier
National Park; Acadia, Maine; and Eugene, Oregon.

Even after she was diagnosed, she stayed astonishingly active—
continuing to walk and bike through all of the exhaustive treatments:
the months of chemotherapy and the pair of clinical trials that she had
to cross state lines to participate in. She was back out on her snowy dirt
road just over a week after her initial surgery. Her thick L.L.Bean boots
leaving soft imprints of determination in the fresh dusting of snow. She
continued to walk with her friends every single day of recovery. And
soon she was peppering in bike rides again, getting out as often as her
treatments' harsh side effects allowed. She even biked forty miles three
months before the end of her life.

We never expected to be mourning her at sixty-six, just a year after
she retired from a forty-two-year career as a public schoolteacher. She was
supposed to be running marathons and biking to all the covered bridges
in Vermont well into her nineties.

But cancer is anything but judicious or fair, so here we were, in a small
hospice home on the outskirts of Burlington, Vermont, discussing the
deterioration of senses in the waning hours of life.

The nurse tucked my mom's feet under the navy fleece blanket and
offered me a comforting smile as she walked out of the room.

"Call me if she needs anything," she said, easing the door shut behind her.

My brother rose from the green couch in the corner of the room and stumbled to my side. Neither of us wanted to chance being away from her when that last breath arrived, so I'd slept on the armchair beside her bed, and he'd slept on the couch beneath a light waffle blanket he found in the closet—or gotten as close to sleep as you can while frantically listening to the sounds of labored breathing. Second-guessing each and every noise that broke the stillness of night. The threat of missing any gasp signifying the end of our mother's life was an anti-sleep drug.

Jameson lowered his tall body close to her bed and clasped her hand in his, letting his head fall toward our mother. All the gravity in the room pulled toward her.

The signature characteristics of my mom's face were already fading. Her glasses gone. Her Irish skin even paler than normal. Her piercing blue eyes that matched ours hidden behind shuttered lids. Her sly grin, a sidekick to her quiet humor, limp and flattened.

"I love you so much, Mom," Jameson choked out. His words were as choppy as Lake Champlain on a gusty morning.

I felt a sob swelling in my throat.

We'd been navigating the grim reality of our mother's aggressive cancer for over a year, but uttering words that acknowledged her rapidly approaching death was what made it feel as real as my racing heart. Her death was about to shift from a murky question to a cold, hard fact.

And it was when our voices cracked the air with final goodbyes, that the imminence of losing her hurtled toward me like a runaway train. I held my mother's hand, trying to soak up the dwindling heat of her skin, clinging to the faint beat of her pulse. Asking myself the same question over and over and over: What do you say while you still have the chance?

Five months before I was in that hospice room, staring down the barrel of my mother's death, I was running 100 miles through the Cascade Mountains that skirt the sleepy town of Easton, Washington. My morning had started outside the brick red fire station in the town center alongside 150 other runners sporting race bibs and hydration packs. Wispy clouds floated overhead as we crossed the start line on the quiet dirt road.

It was my third time doing this particular race—the Cascade Crest 100—and my fifth time tackling the 100-mile distance on foot.

As I climbed up a rocky trail that shoots to the top of the course's highest peak, I started thinking about that collection of 100-mile runs and how much my relationship with them had changed over the last few years.

I'd finished my very first 100-miler six summers ago, and it had felt so different from later ones, where my steps were infinitely more confident. Where both my body and mind found ease through the inevitable fatigue that hits during 100 miles of human-powered travel.

That inaugural crack at triple-digit mileage was, by far, the hardest thing I'd ever attempted. No part of me was at ease for a single mile of the race. My heart rate crested triple digits before we even started running. When I'd crossed that start line in Southern Oregon in a sea of headlamps, I had no idea if I could actually cover 100 miles with my own two feet and make it all the way to the finish line.

That uncertainty defined so much of the run. And was why I'd wanted to tackle the distance in the first place.

I'd done plenty of long-distance trail running and racing before I signed up for that first 100-mile run—with a number of 50ks and 50-milers under my belt. But a 100-miler was a different beast. It would mean running straight through the night and well into the next day. Moving forward over mountains for over twenty-four hours with zero minutes of sleep. Contending with the extra-challenging variety of problems that pop up during such a ridiculous volume of miles and hours. Hammered quadriceps. Debilitating stomach issues. Trailside hallucinations. Blisters the size of silver dollars.

I debated registering for the Pine to Palm 100 Mile Endurance Run in Southern Oregon for months. It was ultimately a curiosity about whether I could actually run 100 miles that motivated me to sign up.

The question mark that punctuated that goal was terrifying—in the most alluring way. I wanted to be trying things that felt at least a little unachievable. Things that unleashed an army of butterflies in my stomach. And that was exactly what the Pine to Palm 100 did. As I hovered my finger over the bright green register button on the race's sign-up page, I felt thousands of winged nerves swarming me from the inside out.

My most reliable training partners in the months leading up to Pine to Palm were uncertainty and an excited fear. And I loved their constant presence in my miles around the wooded trails of Eugene and the foot-hills of the Cascades.

They reassured me that I was running toward the edge of my limits—and trying to see if I could keep going. That I was chasing an opportunity to surprise myself with the depth of my strength and resil-ience. That I was on those trails for all the reasons I was a runner in the first place. Because I wanted to explore just how much I could do—and try to redefine that again and again.

Just like I'd watched my mom do for years.

My mother was every reason I became a runner.

When I was growing up, my mother had been moderately active—but not especially so. We'd go on a few hikes and visit a handful of bike paths every summer, but these jaunts were a way to introduce us to enriching experiences, not because she was so devoted to physical activity. She was the type of mom who helped us create scrapbooks after family vacations to Maine and toted us around to random corners of Vermont to participate in educational tours of historic landmarks. A third-grade teacher, in and out of the classroom.

But after she was hospitalized for a gallbladder removal when I was a teenager, her relationship to exercise changed. When I visited her and found her lying in bed, wrapped in the sanitized whiteness of hospital sheets, I could tell something in her was shifting. She gazed out the window, her face showing a resolve I hadn't seen before.

When she was released from the hospital, she decided to make some changes for herself. Her health scare motivated her to move from a sedentary lifestyle to one that involved more activity.

She started walking. Just a mile at a time at first. She'd leave our family home in rural Vermont and before the minute hand had ticked halfway around the clock, we'd see her walking back up our long, winding driveway, her bobbed brown hair bouncing with each stride. Each footfall was heavy with effort as she climbed past the maple saplings that lined the driveway like sentries, her hard work on display through the white-paned windows.

As she got stronger, she started tackling progressively longer distances—soon making her way to various 5ks and 10ks around Vermont, first participating as a walker, then pushing the speed of her stroll in the race walk division. I tagged along to these events and watched as my mother evolved into an excited athlete and unstoppable woman. Her arms and legs pumping with determination through every mile.

Eventually, her quick walk morphed into running—and soon she climbed the ladder of distances: 5ks, then 10ks, a half marathon, and when she turned fifty, she decided she was going to run her first full marathon.

I wasn't much of a runner myself yet. I admired her from the sidelines as she collected colorful race bibs that she hung on the refrigerator and scrapbooked as we had our childhood trips around New England. She filled my teenage years with powerful displays of just how much can be gained from pushing our limits and redefining what we can do.

When she toed the line at the Vermont City Marathon in 2004 for her first 26.2-mile run, I was nineteen years old and in awe of what my mother was doing with running. I chased her around the course to cheer her on all morning. She bounced through the neighborhoods and lakefront paths of Burlington with a huge grin on her face. My voice was scratched raw from yelling so hard, and my fingers were blistered from ringing a cowbell for over four hours as she ran a marathon around the biggest city in Vermont.

When she took her final steps toward the rainbow of ribbons lining the finish, I jumped and cried like a high school cheerleader, overwhelmed with excitement for my mom.

I ran through the crowds to congratulate her. She emerged through the chaos of the finish, sporting a medal with the Vermont City Marathon logo. That same giddy smile stretched across her face. Her joy shone through the 26.2 miles of fatigue.

"You're a marathoner!" I cried, as I jumped and threw my arms around her.

I had never felt so proud of my mom.

It was impossible to walk away from watching her finish her first marathon as a fifty-year-old woman and not feel wildly inspired to run one myself

So, a few years later, I did just that.

"I'm going to run a marathon, just like you!" I announced, as I walked into the kitchen of my parents' house during a break from my last semester of college.

"Which one?" she fired back. Excitement buzzed through her question. Her eyes lit up. She was still wearing a pink running shirt and long black shorts from her morning miles. I knew she was going to run that marathon with me as soon as I told her my plan.

She was on her fourth marathon by the time we flew to DC at the end of October 2007 so we could run the Marine Corps Marathon together. Or rather, run at the same time. We didn't actually run a single mile together as she proceeded to cruise ahead and beat me by twenty minutes, while I discovered just how hard it is to finish a marathon.

I was jittery with nerves at the start, bouncing up and down in the crowd of 30,000 runners. But it grounded me to stand beside my mother, thinking about how she'd done this three times before. I remembered the woman who could barely walk a mile, who now had her fourth marathon bib pinned to her shirt.

"You're going to run a marathon today, Emily," she said, as she squeezed my hand during the final minute before we took off.

The first few miles were a breeze, and I ran way faster than I should have, just like my mom warned me not to do. And then my legs flooded with fatigue as I ran past the Lincoln Memorial and the Washington Monument during the second half of the race. Each mile got harder and it started to feel impossible that I'd find enough in me to make it all the way to the finish line.

As lead pulsed through my limbs, I thought about my mom—going from walking a mile to running four marathons—and I pushed through the exhaustion. I found the hidden gear of strength that my mother promised I could. And I kept going right past the Jefferson Memorial and across the Potomac River. I made it all the way to the final monument, where a gauntlet of Marines cheered me through my last very tired steps into the finish line chute.

When I found my mother through the crowd, I was wearing my own marathon medal, that same giddy smile now on my face. I was in disbelief and awe that I'd finished something that had seemed impossible for so many steps of the race. That I'd done the thing my mom had inspired me to try.

Her smile stretched across her salt-crusted face, beaming with motherly pride and excitement that we now shared this thing that had become so important to her. She wrapped me and my foil heat sheet in a big hug.

"I'm so happy we did this," she said.

"I'm so happy you inspired me to," I told her, and let my tired face fall to her shoulder.

It was that 26.2-mile tour of the nation's capital that hooked me on the sport. After that first marathon, I followed in my mother's footsteps and eagerly tackled the increasingly tough goals that running offers.

I loved asking myself, "Can I actually do this very hard thing?" as I chased both progressively tougher speeds and distances—through running marathons, then faster marathons, then long-distance trail races and runs, double crossings of the Grand Canyon, and colossal loops around the biggest volcanos in the Pacific Northwest.

Now I was running my fifth 100-miler through the mountains around Easton, while my mom was going through cancer treatment back in Vermont.

And while I was climbing my way to the top of the Cascade Crest course, I recognized that I was no longer chasing that exciting uncertainty or fear that had drawn me into the sport in the first place and had defined so many of the goals that'd kept me hooked on long-distance running for years. I was no longer pushing myself like my mother had done since I was a teenager.

And I realized that I hadn't been for a while. I gazed out at the endless layers of ridgelines on the horizon and couldn't remember the last time I'd started a run doubting whether I could finish it. As I marched up the long climb to the top of Thorp Mountain, I thought about how much I missed that feeling.

When I'd walked to the start that morning, under a soft August sky, I wasn't afraid of the race. I didn't have 173 questions sprinting through my head like a stock exchange ticker tape. My palms weren't clammy with a nervous sweat. I wasn't spending much mental energy wondering whether I could get to the finish. I knew I could. And I didn't love how confident I'd become about the running goal before me. I didn't love the ease that washed over me as I started running that morning. I didn't love that I didn't see my mother in myself that day.

In the meantime, while I'd been getting entirely too comfortable with everything I did in my running shoes, my mother kept pursuing big and brave things with the reliability of rain in Oregon. She was still running, but she'd also learned how to swim so she could do her first triathlon at the age of sixty. She jumped out of a plane that same year to celebrate her birthday. She had a beaming smile glued to her face for all 10,000 feet of falling through the wide-open sky. She started biking more and would regularly ride seventy-plus miles for a casual weekday tour of New England foliage. And, most impressively, she continued living in a whole-hearted, brave, and truly joyful way through a grim cancer diagnosis.

She refused to let the darkness of cancer completely define her life. She road-tripped to Maine with her girlfriends to attend some Podunk diner's Bald Thursday after she lost her hair from chemotherapy. She went on a sunset lighthouse tour and ate a lobster roll on the beach after finding out that her first round of chemotherapy didn't work. And she actively chased happy days through all of the hardest stretches of her life-threatening cancer.

While I was scaling that trail up Thorp Mountain in the back half of Cascade Crest, my mom was gearing up to start her first clinical trial in Boston—and I realized just how much I was missing that fear and boldness of my earlier running pursuits. And just how much my mother made me want to chase bigger and braver things.

I started to think about the disappointing gap that existed between what I was doing and the kinds of goals she set. And the way she lived. That gap felt as large as the mountains that swallowed the 100-mile course through the Washington Cascades.

My mom had inspired me to start running—and I could feel that fire she stoked reigniting. Especially as she was within months of the end of her life and still doing everything she could to lead a brave and whole-hearted existence. As I kept running toward the finish line, I realized I wanted to attempt a challenge that was bigger and bolder. I wanted to run something that would terrify me in the most exciting way. I wanted to chase a goal that would unleash that army of butterflies. I wanted to be more like my mom.

My brother was now telling my mother all of the things he wanted to do to celebrate her. Bike rides on her birthday. Tours of the covered bridges in Vermont. He told her how great she would be as a grandmother. How he couldn't imagine not seeing her with the kids he might have someday. He looked at her with the bright blue eyes that matched hers. Her eyes still sealed shut.

I sat there listening, mulling my own last gasps of love and the final promises I wanted to share with my mom.

I stroked the back of her hand with my thumb—letting the rhythm of our touch fill the silence.

I took deep breaths to brace myself for the challenge of speaking to my mother for one of the final times. I felt every word catch in my throat—afraid of what releasing them acknowledged.

I was never going to be ready to say goodbye to her.

No words could capture my fierce love for my mother. No words could convey how scared I was to know a world without her. No words could change the irreversible nightmare that was hurtling toward us.

No words would ever feel like enough. But we kept talking to her anyway. No matter how little I wanted to accept the cruel fate we were facing, I knew I would regret not saying a goodbye that reflected the love between us.

I told her I loved her. I took another deep breath.

"I'm going to miss you so much, Mom." Each word felt like it was falling off a cliff. "I don't know how to keep living without you."

And then I leaned down and told her I was going to do something big and brave for her this year. Just like she'd inspired me to do when I started running. And will always inspire me to do.

"I'm going to run across Oregon on the Pacific Crest Trail—to celebrate the bravest woman I've ever known," I whispered.

Saying the words out loud triggered the panic I knew they would. I swallowed through the lump in my throat and squeezed back tears so I could keep looking at her face. I didn't want to lose a second with her.

No goodbye to my mom would ever feel like enough. No goodbye could ever make any of this feel okay. But there was a little glimmer of peace in letting her know I will always find ways to remember her. And to hold her close.

And then I told her I loved her. Again and again.

I choose to believe that she heard everything I said.

One

RUNNING NORTH

AUGUST I, 2020
DAY ONE—CALIFORNIA BORDER TO KENO ACCESS ROAD
62.8 MILES, 8,947 FEET OF CLIMBING

Mile 1,
Siskiyou Mountains

I start running to the Gorge beneath a charcoal sky. The Oregon Pacific Crest Trail (PCT) will carry me 460 miles from the dry hills that rise above the California border to the dramatic Columbia River Gorge, where the massive Columbia River unfurls through a deep canyon and carves a border between Oregon and Washington.

The early morning wraps me in crisp air as I try to settle into a pace that I can sustain for the next 460 miles.

As that number floats into my head, I feel a rush of fear wash over me. That is a stupid amount of miles, I think. I've never run more than 100 miles in one go in my life. What the hell am I trying to do out here? How do I cover the entirety of Oregon on foot? That is definitely not something I know how to do. That is definitely not something I know I can do. I might as well have decided I would learn to fly so I could hitch an afternoon breeze to Alaska.

"Don't think about the number of miles!" I scold myself, actually vocalizing my internal monologue to the dark trail. "One step at a time, Emily."

I can't shake the monstrous number from my head, but my feet obey and keep churning forward with a metronomic rhythm. As the ground ticks by beneath my legs, I start to settle into a steady stride. I draw in deep breaths of the cool dawn air and try to shed some nerves as I run.

The sky is waking up on the eastern horizon, tickling the edge of the mountains with a tangerine glow. The silhouettes of the cedars that line the trail shift into focus as I dart between flower-flooded meadows and sparse forests.

"What a gorgeous morning," my boyfriend, Ian, calls from behind me. He is pacing me through the first few miles of the run to save me from starting in the dark by myself. It's not the dark I mind so much as the mountain lions that roam the forests during the dim bookends of the day. His presence makes me feel safer as I run through their hunting ground, scanning the shadows for glowing eyes.

I take another deep breath and savor the soft sky and the rolling hills, letting the serene wilderness ground me in the moment.

"It really is beautiful," I say.

It feels right to start the run with Ian—he'd been such a huge part of the planning and preparation for this run. And I'd needed the help. The logistics of running across an entire state were nearly as daunting as the run itself—the maps, the mileage, the crew stops, the sleep spots, the water sources, the food, the gear, the pacers, the plans B through Z. There was so much to map out, and planning is not my forte. I would take 460 miles of running over logistics any day. But it's hard to run across an entire state without a list or two, so I begrudgingly compiled a few spreadsheets and lists to feel ready for this run. Or, at least to feel as ready as possible when venturing into a trek full of so many unknowns.

I remember when I first became aware that this run was a thing that people did. It was back in 2013, when Brian Donnelly, an elite trail runner from Portland, set a speed record on the stretch of the PCT that travels across the entire state of Oregon. I stumbled upon his run report on the internet and devoured it, lingering on every detail of his seven days, twenty-two hours, and thirty-seven minutes of running, the fastest anyone had ever traveled Oregon's PCT. In the trail-running world, we label record-setting runs like Brian's as Fastest Known Times—or FKTs, which is exactly what it sounds like. These are not races in the usual sense, but rather when someone—sometimes alone, sometimes with a support crew—travels a stretch of trail faster than anyone else has done. Runners have chased FKTs on iconic trails all over the country and the world—from the Grand Canyon to the Appalachian Trail to the PCT.

It was such a cool idea for a run, I thought, as I read Brian's report. To cover all of Oregon on foot. To embark on a slow-cooked tour of its most stunning landmarks—Crater Lake, Mount Hood, the dramatic arc of the Cascade volcanos. Moving past each of these mammoth geological footprints one step at a time. As I read Brian's recap, I imagined doing it myself someday. But then I did the math on how many miles he ran each day, which averaged 57.5, and laughed at my foolish fantasy. It was too big for me. Even trying to do it in twice the time he took would be a ginormous undertaking, demanding more than a marathon a day for over two weeks.

And now I was out here, seven years later, trying to beat Brian's time.

I was a different runner now than I was seven years ago, for sure. I'd run five 100-milers and plenty of big, self-supported adventure runs in that time. To cover so many miles in a day felt slightly more achievable. But this goal was still more than a little outlandish—especially going for the overall record—trying to beat the men's mark alongside that of the women. Plenty of competitive men had tried to beat Brian's time. Who did I think I was, going for it myself?

"I think this is a record that can be won with grit," I'd told a friend a few weeks ago. "And I've got grit for days. Hopefully for eight of them."

I've never been an athletic all-star with standout results, but I've loved to push myself through sport since I can remember. I was always the kid on the swim team who'd get the "most tenacious" award at the end of the season, a nod to how hard I'd fight for my goals, even if they weren't the flashiest times or places. One of my favorite swim practices was when my coach, Peter, would have us do a set of fast intervals and just when we thought we'd finished the last one, he'd announce we had one more to go, and he wanted it to be our fastest one yet. I loved scraping the bottom of my barrel of strength and realizing I had a little more to give. I've found that this trait goes far in long-distance trail running, when your mind needs to convince your body that it can keep going through the inevitable discomfort and fatigue. I know my grittiness will be one of my greatest attributes during this run, when I'll need my mental strength as much as my physical fitness.

Running across Oregon at any pace would be an incredible feat. But I'd known I wanted to go for the record as soon as I decided to do this run for my mom. I wanted to do something bold enough to scare me, big enough that it would push me to the brink of my limits, uncertain enough that I'd have to risk failure. Just like she did all the time.

At first, I was targeting the women's mark, which is a couple of days slower than Brian's. But as I started mapping out each day of mileage, I found myself drafting a schedule that would put me in a position to beat the men's time as well. As if my subconscious had landed on an even more ambitious goal and didn't feel the need to consult me before committing us both to it. And I went along with it. Allowing the mileage column on my spreadsheet to populate with brazen numbers: sixty today, seventy tomorrow, sixty most every day after that—all the way to Washington.

My grief has been a strange thing. Some days it wrestles me to the ground and pins me down with so much force that I can't move from my bedroom floor. And other days it drives me to run up and down mountains. To sprint until my lungs are on fire. And to map out the most ambitious run of my life.

This goal to run across Oregon, and to do it for my mom, has been one of the only things that could get me out the door on some of the hardest days since her death. And when running helps me move through grief, it's hard not to feel like my mom is right there with me, helping me through the pain of losing her.

My plan is to get to the Columbia River Gorge at the other end of the state by next Saturday night—less than eight days from now, so I can compete with Brian's record.

Eight days of running is the next number that lodges itself in my brain as I keep jogging beneath a pastel sky. I am on an open ridgeline and the horizon is a layer cake of mountains: the Trinity Alps, Mount Shasta, the Siskiyous.

Brian wrote that he had run for sixteen to seventeen hours each day. Sleeping just a few hours a night before packing his bag and doing it again day after day. That's my plan as well. To run to each of my planned stops for the night—where Ian's van will be parked and ready for me to crash for a few hours, with a memory foam mattress topper shoved onto a wooden platform in the back and covered with sleeping bags. And then I'll wake up, chug a cold can of coffee, tape up my blisters, and do it all again.

Another wave of panic slams into me. I've only been running for an hour. The immensity of trying to run across the entire state of Oregon sucks the air out of me. I try to breathe through it and settle into the act of running. This small strip of dirt will be my home for the next eight days.

I look down at the trail and remind myself that this is exactly where I want to be.

I've known that this run across Oregon was the run I wanted to do for my mom as soon as I decided to do something to celebrate her life. And to honor how brave she was. It checks all of the right boxes: very big, maybe impossible, and fucking terrifying.

December 2018
Eugene, Oregon

When my mother called me on a late December afternoon, I knew something was wrong right away. My mom was rarely emotional, but I heard her voice crack as she asked me if I had time to talk.

"Of course," I told her—racking my brain for what could possibly be wrong. Someone must've died, I thought. The cat is sick. He's reached his final days, maybe.

"I have cancer," she stammered and then went quiet. I could picture her at our family home in Vermont. Perched on the green leather stool that I used to sit on every night at dinnertime as a child, with a glass of milk next to my plate. Her body was probably folded into the white countertop, heavy with fear and sadness. Maybe she was nervously swiveling a little, creaking her seat slowly from side to side as she waited for her daughter to respond to the unimaginable news that she had just dropped into the phone from 3,000 miles away.

I sank against the bedroom wall and fell to the floor. My body found the carpet below. My limbs surrendered to the weight of my mother's words. I stayed there for an hour after we hung up, frozen in shock. Unable to move past "I have cancer." I don't remember anything else we said during that phone call. Just "I have cancer," reverberating from Vermont to Oregon and back.

I felt myself float through the days following her diagnosis. My body went through the motions, but I was never wholly there. I was detached from the world around me—unable to engage with my life after learning my mother might be careening toward the end of hers. As if to plug back into my life was to accept this news. To face the threat of losing my mother decades before I expected.

That first phone call ignited a flurry of increasingly bad news about my mother's prognosis.

"It's a rare and aggressive uterine cancer," was the next bomb from Vermont. "Papillary serous uterine cancer."

A frantic Google search about this more specific diagnosis didn't help my anxiety or despair.

"What is the survival rate for papillary serous uterine cancer?" I typed. My hands shaking above the keyboard. My heart swallowing my throat. The search engine results lacked empathy or sugarcoating. Google informed me that the survival rate for papillary serous uterine cancer was dismal. It was more likely than not that I wouldn't have a mother

in five years. There was a good chance I would not have a mother a year from then.

That idea was something I couldn't even entertain. My eyes read that statistic and my brain rejected it. The thought of my mother dying within a year was simply unthinkable.

Once her diagnosis progressed into the more specific one, the graver one, everything was fast-tracked. The doctor's urgent concern was terrifying; it was alarm bells blaring, red lights flashing. "Cancel your plans for the next few weeks," her oncologist warned as she tried to squeeze my mom in for surgery during the holidays. She asked if she could still visit New York City with her cousins the next weekend. "I wouldn't," she told my mom.

"We need to do a scan to stage it, but with this type of cancer, it's usually at least Stage 3 by the time a symptom appears," she warned. My mother had gone to the doctor on the very same day as her very first symptom. But it was already too late to catch her cancer before it had advanced.

I spent the week of Christmas trying to numb away every distraught feeling. I drank the most potent IPAs I could find, whiskey drinks with four shots squeezed into the ice, entire bottles of wine. I skied through harsh blizzards, hucking my body onto steep, forested slopes where the only thing I had space to think about was how to turn fast enough to avoid colliding into one of the trees. I filled every moment I could with anyone who would talk to me, who would sit with me, who would save me from thinking about the one thing I couldn't fully face.

I was as fragile as a robin's egg balancing on the edge of a threadbare nest, and to let the reality of my mom's diagnosis hit would yank away the final twig that held me up. I saw myself falling off the edge and shattering into a million pieces. A pile of shards unrecognizable as the thing they once knit together.

Mile 5,

Siskiyou Mountains

I hear Ian's quick steps on the trail behind me. I picture him swiveling his head to take in the beauty that envelops us, flicking his headlamp off as the darkness fades away. His closely buzzed hair covered by a black trucker hat and his muscular thighs slicing through his brightly colored split shorts. Ian is more of a mountaineer, skier, and climber than a runner—but he's a natural athlete and very capable of pacing me for a few miles during these big runs.

"It really is a stunning morning," I say, scanning the ridge before us. The rising sun illuminates the wildflowers lining the thin trail, shrubby golden buckwheat, wild blue flax, tall stalks of lupine. The next meadow hangs on the horizon like a watercolor painting.

We run through a series of meadows. The trail undulates over rolling hills. The sky has shifted from black to pink to blue. Ian ducks off the trail after seven miles together with an excited, "You're doing this, babe!"

I say goodbye with a quick kiss and a few words of gratitude. And I keep running north. I feel like I will be running north forever.

Two hours later, I glance down at my watch.

It reports that I am on mile seventeen.

I can't do the math to calculate what percentage of the run I've finished at mile seventeen, but I don't need to do much arithmetic to know that I've made fairly pathetic progress toward my final destination.

I look up at the horizon and see Pilot Rock perched on the next ridge-line over, a volcanic feature that towers over the surrounding landscape, making it one of Southern Oregon's signature landmarks. The massive monolith of magma had looked as far away as the Washington border all morning—but it will only mark my halfway point for the first day by the time I arrive at the base of it several hours from now. The magnitude of what I am trying to do wallops me again. I wonder if this is how my mom felt during her first marathon. Or her first triathlon. Or when she was perched on the edge of that plane before leaping out of it, on the precipice of a ten-thousand-foot jump. She always seemed so calm and confident, but she probably grappled with more fear than she let on.

A wave of grief smacks into me. An ache gnaws at my chest. I regret never asking her.

I flick my eyes back up at the horizon and think about all the mountains I can't see yet—Diamond Peak, the Three Sisters, Mount Hood—all the major Oregon Cascades that I will need to run up and down and around to get to Washington.

I can feel my legs getting tired, the familiar toll of a long run seeping into my muscles. My steps aren't as springy as they were at the border. I've made piddly progress and I'm already feeling fatigue. I grab a handful of gummy bears from my pack. I have to keep eating to keep moving. To cover sixty miles a day will require thousands of extra calories to give my body the energy it needs.

I think about how tired I will be tomorrow. And the next day. And the one after that. I think about how many of my friends will go to work on Monday morning—two days from now. They will put in a full work week. They will sip coffee and take long showers and have drinks with friends and get eight hours of sleep a night.

And I will just be running.

I think about all the things that could go wrong on this run: cougar encounters, alpine storms, golf-ball-sized blisters, limb-shattering falls, debilitating nausea, navigational mishaps, total failure. I have so many miles to run and so much that could happen between California and Washington.

January 2019
Lincoln, Vermont

I flew to Vermont for my mom's initial surgery. She was instructed to do stairs just once a day and focus on rest. I made her buttered toast and herbal tea and brought her blankets and books. I sat and read next to her while she slept—quietly turning pages while her slow breath rose and fell.

Within a week, she was ready to move again. She started pacing circles around the crackling fireplace that sat in the middle of my parents' home. She reminded her body that it is a body that moves forward. She is a woman who moves. She is a woman who lives. Every single day she can.

My mother used to text me on a near daily basis. "I fucking love retirement," she'd say. The curse an uncharacteristic use of colorful language for her. We were banned from saying words like "sucks" and "shut up" as children. Her rare use of profanity emphasized just how much she really loved retirement. She seized every day of it: biking seventy miles with a girlfriend before noon, reading in a coffee shop—tearing through 160 books during that first year off from teaching, driving through the night to another state to see Bruce Springsteen perform, traveling to Glacier National Park to run a half marathon and go whitewater rafting. I was afraid of river sports—but my mom charged rapids with a laughing smile.

On my sixth day in Vermont, it snowed. Fat flakes somersaulted outside the four-paned windows lining every room in the house. We watched the snow pile atop the rows of maple trees and stacks of firewood.

"I want to go for a walk outside," my mother said. She eyed the closet full of thick jackets and fleece mittens. "I'll be careful," she promised, knowing I was nervous about the idea of her pushing too hard. Of falling. Of things getting worse.

I pulled on my own warm layers as she got ready to go outside for the first time since her surgery. Her movements soft, cautious, and eager as she slid her arms into her thick down jacket. She pulled a purple headband over her ears.

We stepped outside and into a winter wonderland. Everything was covered in a blanket of fluffy snow and more flakes flurried from the sky, swirling around us like we were inside a snow globe.

My mom walked a few steps then spun around to take it all in. Each step was careful, but her eyes danced like a child on a snow day.

I watched her. Amazed by how light her spirit was after all the cancer talk and testing and procedures. The hours-long surgery to combat a life-threatening disease. I'd been so steamrolled since her diagnosis, barely able to show up for my days. Fighting off a constant storm of despair. But she was finding ways to insist joy still had a place in her life.

I watched her waft through the snow. Her steps were careful, but giddy. Her gratitude for the beauty of fresh snow shimmering through the heaviness of how sick she was.

Cancer had crashed into her life and erased the promise of her future. A promise that never actually exists for anyone, but that we all want to believe in. That we let ourselves believe in.

But she was shin-deep in snow, immersing herself back in the world that existed beyond cancer.

In some twisted, senseless cruelty of the universe, my mother wasn't the only member of my immediate family dealing with cancer during that trip back to Vermont. My thirty-five-year-old sister-in-law, Jessica, was diagnosed with breast cancer just weeks before my mother.

Jess was the most vivacious woman. You'd never meet her and expect she could get a life-threatening illness, as if that's how cancer works.

She greeted me like we were the best of friends when I met her for the first time, on the lakefront in Burlington, Vermont. The first things I noticed about Jess were her striking beauty and her radiating warmth. She folded me into an excited hug as soon as she walked up, like it was the one-thousandth hug between us. She had big doe eyes and an inviting smile. Her whole face glowed when she was happy. She was impeccably put together when she sat down at our table on the waterfront, in dark skinny jeans, leather boots, and a flowing charcoal sweater.

She was not the kind of woman I tended to befriend. While I spent my weekends running through the mountains and kicking dirt all over my ankles, Jess traveled to New York for fashion shows, picking new items for her boutique clothing shop on Church Street. We didn't have a lot in common, but we both loved my brother. And I immediately loved her when I saw them together. She was so smitten with Jameson. Her hand gently rested on his forearm as we sipped beer and picked at french fries. Her big smile stretched even wider when she looked at him. And she affectionately teased him about their first conversation on Bumble as she told me about how they met.

"I was too nervous to like his profile," she said. "So, I threw my phone across the room. But then I panicked that I wouldn't find him again."

I know Jameson felt like he was dating out of his league with Jess. "But Jess feels the same way," my mom told me over the phone before I flew home to meet her. And it was obvious, being around them, that they each felt like the luckiest person in the world to be with the other.

It didn't make any sense when Jess was diagnosed with breast cancer just two months before my mom. She was too young. Too full of life and a dreamy future with Jameson. Their wedding was as impeccably put together as Jess always was. It was clear she'd been planning it since she was old enough to throw a pillowcase over her hair and pretend it was a veil. I'm not really much of a wedding person, but I bawled at theirs, bowled over by how much love radiated around them.

Jess loved fairy tales, and it felt like we were watching her live out her own as she danced into the night with my brother.

But Jess found the lump in her breast the morning after the wedding. She was officially diagnosed within weeks, right after she turned thirty-five. When I flew to Vermont on January 2 to help my mother recover from her surgery, my sister-in-law was starting chemotherapy. Seeing Jess and Jameson was dictated by how she was feeling as she faced her own harsh side effects from the aggressive treatment.

My immediate family was so small. Just me, my brother, my parents, and Jess. And cancer had become such a huge part of our tiny group. Such a grave threat to our existence.

On that trip to Vermont, I drove the quiet highway between my parents and my brother and Jess. The stark landscape of the thirty-mile drive between the two houses was the one space where cancer didn't fester in a body next to mine. Where cancer wasn't lurking beneath the same roof overhead.

It was hard to believe that the last time I was in Vermont, we'd all been at Jess and Jameson's wedding, and no one had been diagnosed with cancer. It was just five months ago. But it felt like another lifetime.

Jess had wanted hours of dancing at the wedding. The band took the stage as the appetizers were dropped on the tables. Jess rushed the floor, and we all charged after her, our heirloom tomatoes forgotten and soggy. After the band played their last song, we piled into vans and moved to her family's camp on the lake and kept dancing until we were flirting with the twilight of the next morning. Jess and Jameson sing-shouted together and when the band slowed down, my brother cried as he swept Jess around the floor.

"I think I'll become a wedding dancer during my retirement," my mother announced the next day. Photos from the night before showed her in her royal blue dress that Jess helped pick out, with a wide grin perma-sealed on her face. She and my father signed up for dance lessons that week.

Jess and Jameson moved into a four-bedroom house a few weeks before the wedding. They started talking about kids. I joked about my role as the loose aunt out West, who would serve my nieces and nephews their first IPA and cover their ankles in dirt from the trails we'd wander together.

We were all painting a vision for the future, our brushstrokes bright and full of promise.

Mile 30,

Cascade-Siskiyou National Monument

When I started running from the California-Oregon border that morning, it was just a year and a half after my mother's diagnosis. She had gone from "fucking loving" every day of retirement to taking her last breath in just thirteen months. The unthinkable—losing her within a year of her diagnosis—had become reality.

My sister-in-law's cancer had metastasized and invaded new organs and parts of her body—her brain, her spine, her hip, her liver. I'd lost track of how many times she'd been rushed to the emergency room in the last handful of months. She couldn't walk unassisted and her scans showed nothing but an uncontrollable explosion of cancerous cells. Jess and I were born just months apart. I was thirty-five on the day I started running across the state of Oregon; she was thirty-six, back in Vermont, where she couldn't take a step without help and her doctors couldn't stop the cancer from growing. There was no good reason at all that it was her and not me. There was no good reason at all that it was her, period.

I finally reach the Cascade-Siskiyou National Monument, where Pilot Rock rises from the dry hills. The sun is scorching above me. The browned grass makes the afternoon feel even hotter. The scent of burning soil hangs in the stale air. My throat is scratchy from the dust that I am kicking up as I run.

Water sources are scarce in the hills of the Monument—where the streams have dried up during the heat of summer. I need to refill my water bladder soon since I've been draining it through the hottest hours of the day. I scour every turn in the trail for flowing water. But there is nothing but dry dirt everywhere I look. I still have another thirty miles to cover before I can stop for the day. I inhale a gulp of hot air and my throat itches with thirst.

My legs are getting heavier as they cover more miles. My quadriceps feel like someone has been playing drums on them with a pair of hammers.

I look down as I swing my arms in sync with my stride. A turquoise cord is wrapped around my wrist, threaded through a silver emblem etched with the words "Stay Brave." My mom wore it through every cancer treatment. And I'm going to wear it for every step of this run. A constant reminder of why I am out here.

My mother had a choice about how to live after she was diagnosed: she could let cancer define her life, feel nothing but fear and anxiety, or she could continue to live as she had always lived—in a brave and wholehearted way.

She chose to keep living through cancer. She decided that while cancer may have threatened the number of days she had left, she was still in control of how much she got out of the ones she did have. And if she was going to have fewer days, she wasn't going to let cancer shroud them all in darkness.

She still had plenty of bad days, of course. Hard days. Sad days. Days where she felt scared of cancer. Scared of dying. Scared of leaving us. But she also had beautiful days. Often at the same time. Braided together in a tangle of emotions.

She felt wonder as she looked up at a sky swirling with snowflakes—with the incisions from surgery still throbbing beneath her down jacket.

When I got back to Oregon after that first trip to Vermont to help my mom, I realized I had the same choice. I could let cancer define my life. I could succumb to my fears and sorrow and let them entomb me forever. I could sit at home and feel like a robin's egg at the edge of a spindly branch, afraid to take another breath.

Or I could be like my mother and see cancer as a directive to live while we can, as scared as we may be. Because it can blindside us at thirty-four or sixty-five. Because the fragility of life is real.

I could show up on the California border, seven months after promising my mom I would run 460 miles for her. I could feel overwhelming fear about the idea of running across the entire state of Oregon. Of trying to do it faster than anyone before me. Feel aware of how much could go wrong. Aware of how hard it would be. Aware of how fragile and vulnerable I am. I could feel all of that and keep running to the Gorge.

Two

POSITIVITY IS ON ANOTHER PLANET

AUGUST 2, 2020
DAY TWO—KENO ACCESS ROAD TO CRATER LAKE NATIONAL PARK
72 MILES, 9,324 FEET OF CLIMBING

Mile 84,
Seven Lakes Wilderness

I can't stop thinking about the one thing that I shouldn't think about today.

Danielle is running in front of me—reeling me along with her steady cadence. I watch her footsteps hit the trail. Dust billows beneath her shoes as her feet collide with the ground.

We just left my first major crew stop of the day, where Ian was waiting with fresh socks, a new pair of shoes, and triangles of quesadilla smothered in guacamole. My friend Jameson, who bizarrely shares a name with my brother, paced me through the day's first twenty miles, and now Danielle is running thirty-four miles with me, before Ian takes over for the last sixteen miles into the outskirts of Crater Lake National Park. None of my friends will be running an insignificant distance today—and I'll be stringing all three of their pacing stints together to get through one monster day.

A seventy-mile day.

Just thinking about it makes me want to stop in the middle of the trail and flag down a helicopter for a ride out of here. Which is exactly why I should stop thinking about how many miles I have to run. I need my brain to help me get through the day—not convince me to bail via an emergency airlift back to my bed.

As soon as I started mapping out this run, it was clear that I either needed to run seventy miles on my first day, or my second, because the crewing and sleeping options through Southern Oregon are so limited.

Or I would fall behind the record before I'd really even started to travel north toward Washington.

I decided the second day would be the lesser of two evils to spare myself such an aggressive start. But now I have a big fat grizzly bear of a day ahead. A bear that lodged itself into the most frontal lobe of my brain as soon as I blinked my eyes open this morning.

My pummeled legs jolted me awake a few minutes before 5:00 A.M. with the shock of tweezers in an outlet. I ran over sixty miles from the California border yesterday and those miles coursed through my limbs like electric currents.

I should not have waited another second to get out of bed as soon as I was conscious. I'll have to run through all the day's light and well into the night to cover today's distance. But I didn't move an inch as I stayed trapped beneath paralyzing overwhelm, tucked in my sleeping bag, shaking my legs and thinking about how far I had to go before I could curl back onto that mattress topper. But when I saw my friend Jameson's headlamp moving around her van, I knew I needed to get going. The seventy miles weren't going to run themselves.

We stepped onto the trail a few minutes after 5:00 A.M., with the beams of our headlamps cutting through the dark morning. Once on the trail, my legs loosened up and I settled into the rhythm of running. I savored the first easier steps of the day, knowing any sense of ease would be fleeting.

And sure enough, that feeling evaporated by the time I left my first big crew stop at mile twenty. I've learned in my many years of ultrarunning that my legs will almost always feel like twenty miles is a long and fatiguing distance, no matter how strong I am. The same way walking up a long flight of stairs can wind me, regardless of how fit I am. And today is no exception. My legs feel the weight of the morning as we jog away from the Summit Sno-park where Ian parked the van.

And now, the grizzly bear of a day has charged back into my head to knock me down.

I have another fifty miles to go before I can stop, I think. *And fifty miles is almost as many miles as I ran *total* yesterday. And I started yesterday fresh and rested.*

And I am 1,000 percent not fresh right now. I've run over eighty miles since starting at 5:30 A.M. *yesterday morning and my legs feel like someone took a jackhammer to my thighs.*

I'm spiraling. All efforts to not think about mileage have gone off the train tracks and are careening out of control.

Danielle spins her head around to check in with me. Her brown ponytail whips through the air.

"How are you doing, Emily?"

Danielle's voice is a hug. She's become one of my most supportive friends, in life and running. She's the kind of friend who just shows up, without me ever whispering a peep about needing her. She calls me on all the hardest grief days. She sends me heart emojis and dog photos when she knows I'm wading through a low. And she checked in every day before I started the run to see if I needed anything and to shower me with encouragement. It's hard to believe I've only known her since I decided to do this eight months ago and reached out to tell her.

Danielle established the women's record on the Oregon PCT last summer. Jameson attempted to do it with her but suffered a foot injury a few days into the run and had to pivot to support Danielle.

I didn't know Danielle at the time, but I remember seeing her share their run when they went after the record last September. Danielle and Jameson were very public about their goal because they wanted their run to encourage more women to chase FKTs. Women are underrepresented in these speed attempts by a rate of around five to one.

"I can't wait for another woman to go after this record," Danielle said in an interview, after successfully finishing the route. "And I hope she calls me up when she decides to do it."

As soon as I decided to be that woman, I knew I wanted to do just that.

I sent Danielle a wordy Instagram message, telling her how much I admired her finish and explaining why I wanted to attempt the record. My heart rate spiked as I sent the message into the internet ether. I was stewing in the vulnerability of sharing such an ambitious goal with a total stranger.

But Danielle didn't make me sit with that anxiety for long. She responded to my message in approximately forty-seven seconds, with at least a dozen exclamation marks punctuating her reply.

"Ahhh!!! That is so great!!! I'm so happy you reached out!!! How can I help? Can I pace you? I'M SO EXCITED FOR YOU!!!!"

Our conversation remained full of exclamation marks and we became fast friends. Danielle offered constant encouragement, accompanied me on many training runs, and gave me advice whenever I needed it.

And now she's here on the PCT with me, crewing and pacing my run—along with Jameson—with all of the expertise they acquired during their 460-mile tour of Oregon.

When I got to my stopping point last night on a dark forest road, Danielle and Jameson charged to my side like a NASCAR pit crew.

I emerged from the woods a little after 9:30, and Danielle rushed through the black night to usher me into the reclining camp chair they brought with them.

"Sit down!" Danielle commanded, her hand on my shoulder, guiding me into the seat.

I eased my body into the chair and Danielle covered me with a sleeping bag because she knew what I needed without me saying a thing. The sun had set and my core temperature plummeted with it. I'd ended the run with beads of sweat on my skin, but as soon as I stopped, I was shivering in my wet clothes.

Jameson immediately started untying my shoes and fearlessly stripped off the socks that were caked in fifty-nine miles of trail and body grime. She palmed my feet and craned her neck so she could examine them from every angle.

"Your feet look pretty good," she said, without an ounce of sarcasm.

I looked down at them. A thick layer of dirt along my socks looked like a tan line. I was missing a handful of toenails. And the remaining ones were bruised or had bits of black soil jammed beneath them.

"Are we looking at the same pair of feet?" I laughed.

Danielle grabbed a baby wipe and started wiping me down.

"Ian! Do you have warm clothes for her? Let's get this girl changed."

"Where's the dirty clothes bag?" Jameson asked.

I laughed again. There was no dirty clothes bag.

Danielle yanked off my sweaty tank top and sports bra so she could dress me in a dry sweatshirt and sweatpants. These two women had mastered the art of multiday monster running. And here I was, floundering around with soiled feet and no laundry bag, while someone else took off my shoes and dressed me for bed, like an overtired toddler.

Danielle handed me a bowl of ramen and I spooned the broth to my mouth. Its steam billowed in my face—I looked around and savored the warmth of such generous support.

And now we're on the trail together, twenty-five miles into the day, and Danielle is still looking at me—waiting for me to respond to her "how are you doing" check-in.

"I'm great," I tell Danielle.

She can see right through my fib.

"I'd already cried like eight billion times by this point," she said. "So much crying on day two! Just raining tears all over this trail."

She throws her hands to the sky and laughs at the memory.

"I actually haven't cried yet," I say. "But I'm sure it's coming."

"Have you been thinking about your mom?" she asks, in her soft and inviting Danielle way.

I know she's not asking that question because she wants to see me cry. I know she's asking because my mom is why I'm here. Because every step of this run is a celebration of my mother's life and a way to move through the grief of losing her. But her kindness and the mention of my mom—on top of my mounting fatigue—trigger hot tears to my face.

I pinch my eyes tight to trap them in. I stop in the middle of the trail with my eyes squinched shut. Danielle hears my footsteps cease and turns around to check on me. When I open my eyes and see her compassionate gaze, I lose it.

I start sobbing. My breath is choppy and desperate. Tears fall onto the dusty soil beneath my feet. I don't know what's grief and what's overwhelm, it's all spilling out of me in a mess of emotions.

Danielle jumps to my side and wraps me in a tight hug. I let my exhausted body fall into her arms and heave into her shoulder. We stand there, me crying, Danielle rubbing the small of my back, until I hear voices approaching from around the corner.

I choke back a sob and look up. Two hikers are walking toward us, staring right at me. My face flushes hot. My eyes are blotchy and my skin is red and puffy. I'm not surprised to be crying in front of Danielle, but I wasn't expecting to crumble before total strangers. My deep-seated instinct is to hide my grief from people outside my closest circle. To run into the bathroom when I feel tears brewing. To squeeze back my emotions when I'm on a plane to Vermont. To almost never provide an honest answer to "how are you doing?" while I'm wading through the thick of it. I've felt the ways society wants me to stuff my hardest feelings down and spare others from the discomfort of being anywhere near them.

And the disruption of seeing people on the trail is enough to stop my tears, at least for now.

The hikers walk by us with an awkward wave. I avert my gaze and mumble a sloppy hello.

"We should keep running," I say to Danielle, rubbing my eyes dry with the back of my hand.

Danielle starts moving down the trail with me.

"Do you want to tell me any stories about your mom?" she asks.

Huge fir trees tower over us. Their limbs stretch into a piney canopy, casting shadows across the thin trail. I find the sky between the branches. I hold onto the sliver of sunlight as we start running.

"Have I told you about Bald Thursday?" I ask.

"No!" she yips. "Go on."

I sigh.

"This is one of my favorites."

My mom lost her hair during chemotherapy, and at first she was embarrassed about her bald head, so she wore beanies whenever she left the house. She ordered new ones from Skida and Turtle Fur by the half dozen so she could rotate through new colors and prints. Lilac on Wednesday. Cobalt on Thursday. Daisies on Friday.

But, one day, she called me and said she was sick of fear having so much control over her.

"I'm going to the gym today," she said. "My goal isn't to go farther or faster but to go bald."

So, she went and sported her baldness while she walked on the treadmill. She said she was still uneasy, with nothing standing between her bald head and the world, but she was proud of herself for being brave.

"I did it—and next time it should be easier," she said.

She started leaving the house without a beanie more and more. And then, as her courage mounted, she decided to take her head back from cancer—and to squash the fear and shame it had made her feel.

She called up two of her girlfriends and invited them on a road trip to visit a rural town in Maine. She'd seen a local diner advertise a Bald Thursday special and decided to celebrate her newfound courage with a 30 percent discount on her coffee, eggs, and home fries. So, they drove several hours north and enjoyed a bald breakfast on a random Thursday morning.

There is a photo from that day of my mom cackling with laughter in a vinyl booth, with a white ceramic coffee mug in front of her—and a plate piled high with potatoes and toast. Her bald head is out and her face is radiant.

"She was genuinely having the time of her life that day," I tell Danielle. "Cancer took her hair—but she refused to let it take all of her joy."

The photo from the diner is hung up on my refrigerator back home. I picture her laughing smile and the memory tears into my heart. I would do anything to see her smile again. To feel its warmth. Fat tears roll off my cheeks and splatter across the trail, leaving damp marks in the dirt. I rub at my swollen eyes with balled-up fists.

Danielle turns and I can see her eyes are watering, too.

Sometimes the fact that I can never see my mom again cracks me open with longing. And right there, in the middle of the Seven Lakes Wilderness, I cracked.

Mile 94,
Seven Lakes Wilderness

The trail grinds uphill and I grind with it. The sun burns hot overhead. Salt clings to my skin as sweat pools and dries on my body. I dig my poles into the earth to help me climb. But my legs feel like there are steel anchors strapped to my ankles. With each step I have to push through the resistance of fatigue, like post-holing through knee-deep snow.

In a moment of tired weakness, I do something that I know will not help: I look at my watch.

The mileage on my watch face beams back at me: 33 miles.

That number is a fast slap in the face.

I am not even halfway through this day, I think. *My legs are pummeled and I'm beyond ready to be done, and I'm not even halfway there.*

I start doing mental math to try to spin the numbers into something more hopeful. But none of it helps. Every spin attempt just makes me feel worse. Because every calculation ends with nearly forty miles to go.

And there is no way to make me feel better about that.

"Snack time!" Danielle cries. She's been a dutiful snack sheriff all day, making sure I force food into my body every thirty minutes. Normally, snacks are one of my favorite love languages. But today, they are repulsive. The combination of the heat and the distance has left my stomach soured on the idea of eating.

I dig into my hydration pack and pull out a baggie of peanut butter pretzels. I pop one into my mouth and chew it a dozen times before I can bring myself to choke down the dry bits. Danielle is watching my every move like a hawk.

"You need to eat a hell of a lot more than a single pretzel." She shoots me a warning glare.

"I know, I know, I know," I whine. "But eating is very hard."

I scrunch my nose at the bag of pretzels.

"Emily," Danielle starts, as if she is scolding a child. "Eating is your job today. Eating is your job for the next seven days. It doesn't matter whether you want to do it, it doesn't matter whether you feel like it, you have to do it."

I sigh and grab another three pretzels and get to work. She is right, I need thousands of extra calories a day to give me enough energy to keep running, but I'm ready to nominate eating over sewer cleaning and pest control on a "worst jobs in the world" list. I wash down the dry pretzel crumbs with a giant slug of water.

I look up and take in the trail ahead of us. The rocky hills jut into the bright sky. I can see the thin strip of trail meandering up through the rocks. The next climb looks like it stretches into eternity. A pika darts into a pile of boulders. I think about following it into its hiding place and burrowing away from this day.

"I think I need to play music," I announce to Danielle. "Really poppy music."

I take out my phone and pull up a downloaded playlist on Spotify. I break my own rule to never use speakers in the wilderness and start blaring Lizzo. I can usually count on Top-40 beats to infuse some energy into my stride.

Lizzo starts wailing about fucking it up to the tempo. She's giving me a play-by-play of how to make it through this day.

I plead with my body to respond. "C'mon, legs. Fuck some shit up. Just a little."

But I'm not fucking anything up. This trail is the one doing all the fucking. My legs are heavy and this climb is endless and I will never be done running ever again.

A wave of defeat brings me to a complete stop in the middle of the trail. I slump down into my poles, letting my full weight hang toward the ground in a bow of surrender. The poles dig into my armpits as I lean into them. I fantasize about the rocks beneath my feet turning into an escalator and carrying me to the top of this mountain.

Danielle is ahead of me and she stops and turns when she realizes my footsteps have gone silent.

"How are you doing, girl?" she asks.

"Day two is really long," I sigh. I try to stay positive during these long runs and adventures, and I pride myself on being able to do just that through some serious lows, but I can only force so much in this moment. I left my positive attitude back in my sleeping bag.

"Day two sucks!" she agrees. "I cried so much on day two. I was bawling by now. You are doing so great. You are doing so much better than I was doing at this point."

I feel my legs buckle beneath me with fatigue. My brain is mushy with bad math.

"I find that very hard to believe," I say. "I was just begging Mother Earth to turn this trail into an escalator."

Danielle cackles. "And she hasn't done it yet? What a bitch."

"If she hadn't made this trail so damn pretty, I'd disinvite her from my run," I go on. A hint of a smile cracks through my misery.

Danielle seizes the glimmer of an opportunity to talk me off my ledge of defeat.

"Okay, what feels the hardest right now?" she asks. "Let's tackle it."

"I have so many miles left," I whimper. "This day is so big and it hasn't stopped being big. No matter how far I go, there is still so much left to run."

She nods. She gets it. I know she gets it.

She has been on this exact patch of trail, drowning in her own sea of fatigue and hopelessness. With entirely too many miles to go.

Danielle pulls out her phone and uses her fingers to zoom in on the satellite map that she downloaded before we started.

"There is a water source in seven miles," she says. "Let's just focus on the next seven miles. That's like an easy weekday run!"

"Maybe it's *your* easy weekday run. I'm more of a five-mile girl."

She giggles, orders me to eat, and cajoles me to keep moving up the hill.

"Let's just get to the next water source," she says.

A lot of ultrarunners use the same trick to get through long races: "Just take it aid station to aid station," everyone says. The idea is to prevent yourself from getting too overwhelmed by the monstrosity of the whole thing. Every run happens step by step, and it's a lot easier to think about taking just that next step or two than a million of them.

This is what Danielle is trying to do. She is trying to coax me away from the numbers in my head, so the next few miles are easier to digest. She's throwing me a life preserver to save me from sinking to the bottom of my mental sea. But it royally backfires.

Seven miles feels like an eternity. And even though I'm not supposed to be thinking about this, I know that the next stretch after the water source is another seven miles. And that feels like an even longer eternity.

And then I have at least sixteen miles with Ian until I can stop for the night. Which means I will basically be running until the end of time.

"Just a weekday run!" Danielle yips. She's trying to pull me into a better place. But I'm stuck in my pit of despair. I can't see this day as anything other than an impossibly hard day. The day's mileage is quicksand and it's pulling me deeper and deeper down.

January 2019
Eugene, Oregon

When my mom was first diagnosed, it was with the wrong cancer.

When she went to her primary care physician on the day of her first symptom, post-menopausal bleeding, her doctor immediately ordered a biopsy.

Her test results came back a few days later. Another doctor told her that she had endometrial cancer.

"If you're going to get cancer, this is the kind that you want to get," her doctor said. "It's highly curable."

But a week and a half later, her medical team realized they'd made an error. She didn't have endometrial cancer. They called her back to their office. She actually had papillary serous uterine cancer, they said, a rare and aggressive cancer that's usually in an advanced stage by the time it's caught. Survival rates are low. Treatment options are scarce.

This time, no one told her it was a better cancer than others.

When she called me with the news on December 18, my housemate, Eli, was packing for a two-week trip to Yosemite. I could hear him piling backpacking gear, freeze-dried food, and his puffiest down jacket on the couch as he got ready to leave. I walked downstairs and scanned the piles. It looked like he was taking half the house with him. He kept stacking gear higher. I thought about how empty our home was about to feel.

My boyfriend at the time, Mark, was getting on a plane to Hawaii the next morning. "I'll text you," he said, as hot tears streamed down my face in a dim taqueria that night.

Meanwhile, many of my other friends were packing their own suitcases and duffel bags, taking advantage of the holiday break to head to Mexico, Tahoe, and family homes in far-flung corners of the country. It felt like everyone I knew was leaving. Eugene would soon be as empty as the renovated barn that Eli and I shared.

Eli gave me a big hug and walked out, with overflowing tote bags hanging from each shoulder. The door clicked shut. The silence screamed at me from every corner.

I felt like a trapped wolf, alone in a cage with my worst fears.

I grabbed a glass from the cabinet and plopped a big ice cube into the bottom. I poured whiskey until the dark brown liquid swallowed the sides of the ice. I took a sip and savored the burn of the liquor sliding down my throat. A sip turned to two. Two turned into a gulp.

But my fear stayed red-hot, no matter how many ounces of whiskey I drank. Every quiet minute was an open landscape for my fears to rage.

The next morning, I scrolled through my contacts, trying to find any friend in Eugene who I could call so I didn't have to be alone with my pulsing anxiety. I was in total survival mode, grasping for anything and anyone that could get me through the next day, the next minute, the next breath.

I texted Mark and asked if he had a few minutes to talk. I kept checking my phone for his response. Flipping the screen on and off and on again. I didn't hear anything until the next day. I sat on my big red chair, tucked beneath a blanket, my hand trembling.

"Sorry, I was surfing," he said, when he finally responded the next morning. "I'm really trying to enjoy this time with my family."

I went skiing with my friend Audrey the next day. She was exactly who I needed to be around. She didn't look away when I cried on the lift. And she stayed by my side as I hurled my body down forested slopes, trying to distract my brain with thirty-foot-high trees to dodge. But on the other side of every tree was my mother's heightened diagnosis. I drove back down the mountain pass to Eugene, my heart hammering inside my chest, panic stabbing every thought.

I imagined my mother back home in Vermont, in the house she'd set up for Christmas as soon as the calendar flipped to December. Candles on every windowsill. Her mismatched Santa collection lined up on the hutch. Her blue lights on the Christmas tree. "My mom loved blue lights," she told us, as she tenderly hung strands of light on our scrappy Charlie Brown tree every holiday season. She'd been hanging her blue lights every year since her mother died. I could see her sitting in front of the tree in the dim glow. I didn't want to think about how soon I might be talking about her in the past tense, clinging to my own remembrances of her.

Mark called me on the fourth day of his vacation.

I told him I was fighting to get through every day.

"I just don't think you're being positive enough," he sighed. "I can't talk long. We're about to watch a movie."

I hung up and sat on my big red chair, turning his words over in my head. My mother had just been diagnosed with a life-threatening cancer. The survival rates for papillary serous uterine cancer were dismal. The chance I would lose my mother within a year was high. No amount of whiskey or stiff hope cocktail was going to make that better.

Positivity felt like it was on another planet.

Mile 102,
Seven Lakes Wilderness

Danielle and I get to the water source after the longest seven miles of my life. A small brook splices through the trail and tumbles over rocks and pebbles. We stop and filter water into our bladders. An army of mosquitoes swarms us as soon as we slow down. I swat them away with one hand, squeezing my filter between mad swings at the air.

Drip. Drip. Drip. I watch the water trickle into my bladder and feel the pinch of a bug bite. I think about how I would rather curl up here and let the mosquitoes feast on my ravaged body than keep going. The water keeps dripping. It taunts me. There's nothing I can do to make it go faster. Another thing I have absolutely no control over.

We stuff our bladders back into our packs.

"Just another weekday run!" Danielle cries and takes off down the trail. I slog behind her. Time inches by. Tenths of miles crawl like molasses.

After what feels like another twelve-forevers, we finally get to the intersection where Nicole, Tom, and Ian are waiting to crew me with a few backpacks full of gear. Because of the lack of road access through this part of the state, the only way to support this huge chunk of trail is to hike over two miles into the PCT from another trailhead.

Nicole and Tom are seasoned thru-hikers and offered up their backpacking skills to crew me at some of the more remote access points on the trail. When they asked what I wanted them to hike in, I wondered if they might be able to bring me a Jetboil, a small camping stove, to cook hot food.

"And maybe also a blanket and change of socks?" I tentatively threw out. "Would that be too much?"

"Emily!" Nicole cried. "This is what we do for fun! We go hiking with backpacks full of stuff. Load us up!"

And they have delivered on that offer. I survey the scene as we arrive. You would never know the van is parked miles away.

"You are amazing," I sigh with gratitude as I take it all in.

There is a hammock strung between trees. A blanket is spread on the ground, covered in food, extra layers, fresh shoes, and my beloved Jetboil.

I collapse on a log and Ian pulls a puffy blanket around me. We've been sweating through blistering heat all day, but the sun is starting to drop in the sky and as I stop moving, my body temperature drops with it.

"What do you need?" Nicole fires at me.

"Mashed potatoes," I say. I cough. My throat is coated with trail dust. I take a slow slug of water.

Ian pulls out the Jetboil, flicks a lighter, and fires it up. I see him grab a stick of butter, which he'll melt into the instant potatoes to force more calories into me.

"How are you doing?" he asks. He crouches down beside me and gives my knee a quick squeeze.

It's a dangerous question for such a hard day.

"This is a lot of miles," I say. It's the best I can do. I am struggling to stay positive again, and unable to fake my way through my misery.

He nods. I can tell he doesn't know how to make me feel better. Which is understandable, because I'm pretty sure nothing other than a chartered plane to the trailhead would make me feel any better right now.

July 2019
Burlington, Vermont

After my sister-in-law Jess was diagnosed with breast cancer in October 2018, she traveled to Boston to get a double mastectomy and then started a multiweek round of chemotherapy back in Burlington. Her prognosis was good. She was young, she caught it early.

Jameson would send me messages about how Jess was doing after each round of chemotherapy. "All of the lights are off and I'm whispering to the dogs," he texted. "She feels awful. We're trying to make the house as dark and quiet as possible."

She made it through four grueling months of treatment and was deemed cancer-free. Jameson called me in a fit of relieved tears. They celebrated with a walk for breast cancer awareness. Their dogs Willard and Jaxon sported bright pink bandanas that said: "My mom is a cancer survivor." Jameson sent me a photo of Jess hugging both dogs after the walk, her radiant smile as big and warm as ever.

A few months later, Jess had a migraine while she was watching one of Jameson's bike races. And a few days later, she was driving home when she started seeing double on the highway.

She ended up in the emergency room—and soon her body was getting scanned again. Her doctors scoured her imaging for clues about her symptoms.

The answer sent another earthquake through Jess and Jameson's world.

The cancer was back. And it had spread to her brain, spine, hip, and liver. She was immediately admitted to the hospital. My brother could barely talk about it.

Jameson spent days and nights in the hospital, sitting with Jess, and sleeping by her side. He snuck their dogs in to lie with her in the narrow hospital bed. He sent me a picture of Jess's big golden dog Willard tucked beside her, with his goofy ears pointing to the sky, and Jaxon, his beagle mutt, curled into her legs. Jess's long brown hair was still thin from chemotherapy.

The same week that Jess was in the hospital, my mom had a meeting with her oncologist about treatment options. Jameson left Jess's bedside to join. He only had to walk down a few flights of stairs to get there.

I pictured my younger brother, sitting next to our parents, his tall frame slumped into the generic medical office chair, listening to my mom's oncologist rattle off information about various treatments. I could see him watching the doctor with wide eyes, and a scared stare, trying to retain any of it—trying to cram the new information into his head, which was already overloaded with cancer.

He texted me the notes he took. "I don't know if I got everything. I'm so tired of this," he said. "I don't even know what to do."

I could feel his heart breaking from 3,000 miles away—and mine shattered with it. All I wanted was to do something—anything—that could make it better for him. I texted photos of my schnauzer, Brutus. I sent him an angry "fuck cancer" text every morning. I told him I loved him several times a day.

But the cancer raged on. Jess got sicker. Our mother's options dried up. As much as I wanted to help my brother, nothing was going to make it okay that his thirty-five-year-old wife was back in the hospital because cancer had spread all over her body. He slept at the hospital with Jess each night; the dogs stayed with her parents. And their big white house, with the two spare bedrooms down the hall, sat quiet and empty.

Mile 111,
Seven Lakes Wilderness

I am still sitting on the log, and I never want to get up ever again. All 206 bones in my body feel the magnetic force of this seat pulling me down.

I let out a deep sigh. I also just want this day to be over, and I know I have to get up to make that happen.

Ian kneels down and puts one hand on my knee.

"Are you ready?" he asks. He locks eyes with me. His gaze searches for something he can work with.

A sliver of orange sun hangs low in the forest. Night will descend over us soon and we'll be stuck in the dark for hours, when everything feels harder.

"Let's just get this over with," I mutter. I press both palms into the bark and push myself up. My legs buckle beneath me. I've run over fifty miles today—and over 110 since yesterday morning. I'm in new longest-run-ever territory. I'll be here until I reach Washington. If I can make it there.

"You're doing it, Emily," Ian says as we start moving north along the trail.

It's unsurprising that Ian is the one marching into the night with me, while I'm clawing my way through these impossibly hard miles. He's always been this kind of person for me.

I met Ian on the top of a mountain a few years ago. I was ski touring through a raging blizzard, and standing on the summit of Eagle Peak, with fierce wind and snow whipping around me, when I saw someone emerging through the stormy abyss below.

Ian was hiking up the slope, sliding one ski in front of the other to carve out an uphill track through the deep powder. He was wearing a bright orange GORE-TEX jacket and a colorful headband over his ears. He waved at our group as he got closer to the top and saw us milling about the summit.

"Beautiful day out here!" he shouted through the howling wind.

I laughed and waved back.

"Where are you all from?" he asked, as he slid up to our group of three. I wiggled my numb toes inside my ski boots. I should have started moving to warm up. But I stayed planted right where I was.

"Eugene," I said. His blue eyes beamed through the whiteout around us. His scruffy beard scratched the edge of his buff. His athletic frame was confident. His outgoing nature sucked me in.

"I'm from Eugene, too!" He grinned.

"Then why aren't we skiing together?" I fired back. It was an uncharacteristically bold move for me, but the words just flew out of my mouth.

"You should definitely give me your number," he said, as he whipped out his phone. I peeled off my gloves and plugged it in, where it still lives as "Emily, let's ski!"

We didn't really start hanging out for another year, and I dated Mark in the interim. But I ended that relationship a few weeks after his trip to Hawaii. It was clear he couldn't handle my mom's illness and he wasn't willing to support me through it. When I asked for help, he said no, which felt even worse than the disappointment of the illusion of support.

I asked Ian to ski that winter. I think I was desperate for a distraction from cancer, and the cute guy from the Eagle Peak summit felt like he'd deliver. And he did, but he also showed me that he was more than a fun person to ski with. I remember driving back from one of my first outings with Ian—when he asked if it was hard to be so far away from my family in Vermont.

It was February, just a couple of months after my mom was diagnosed with cancer—and I'd gone home for her initial surgery but was missing all the first chemotherapy appointments and felt helpless to support her.

"It's gotten much harder since my mom was diagnosed with cancer," I said. It was the first time I'd mentioned that she was sick to Ian—and I was nervous about revealing that to Ian, as I'd quickly learned that not everyone can sit with that kind of emotional pain.

"I hate being on the other side of the country while she's sick," I choked out. "I wish I was closer so I could support her through her treatment and spend more time with her."

He placed a hand on my shoulder and his voice dropped to a soft whisper.

"I'm so sorry," he said. "I can't imagine how hard that is for you."

Ian immediately signaled to me that he could handle being around pain—and that I didn't have to hide my grief and fear from him. And he continued to be that way through all the cancer and loss. He flew to Vermont to meet my mom when she was at her sickest, to make sure he could while she was still alive. He drove across the country with me when I found out she only had weeks left, manning the steering wheel for hours-long shifts into the middle of the night. And he held me through it all, knowing it meant everything to me to not have to brave it all alone.

And now he's here with me, on one of the hardest and darkest stretches of the run—and he's doing it again. I just can't express my gratitude for him in this moment, when I'm drowning in such a dark low.

When one of my friends is pacing me, I fight to save them from dealing with a sour version of Emily. They're being so generous to run with me—and already have to deal with the many challenges of pacing, like running through the night and trying to get me to eat when I'm secretly stuffing calories back into my pack instead of ingesting them. I don't want to pile a negative attitude on top of that. But I feel less pressure to fake positivity with Ian. I can be my full-on miserable self around him.

So I seize the opportunity to devolve into an even lower place as soon as we take off. And I stay there as the miles inch by.

"How many miles do we have left?" I ask, after we've been running for at least two hours. My voice is high and desperate but I'm too tired to feel any shame at all. I know I will regret my attitude tomorrow. But since it feels like tomorrow will never come, I don't even care.

"It looks like at least another eight," Ian says in an apologetic voice, clearly feeling bad for a thing he has absolutely no control over.

"But that's the same number you said last time," I whine. I'm in full-on toddler mode now.

"It hasn't changed in the last minute, Emily."

I kick the trail in frustration. *Has it really only been a minute? It feels like a millennium.*

"Have you eaten?" I can tell Ian is nervous to say anything to me. I am a sleeping giant and he's whispering outside my cave.

"I hate food," I spit out. It's a race to the bottom of my poorest attitude.

"I know, babe. Food is the worst. But you have to keep eating."

I can see that Ian is a saint. I can see that he's trying to help me. I love him for wanting to help me. And I love him for loving me through the lowest of my lows. And not running away when I'm going through the worst of it. But my gratitude and love for Ian stand no chance against my vitriol against everything else. I hate running. I hate food. I hate this trail. I hate how far we still have left to go before we can stop. And I'm no longer trying to hide any of it.

I take a plastic baggie of mashed potatoes out of my pack and sit on a downed tree. I know this is not going to get me to the end any faster, but I have to stop. The next step feels entirely too hard to confront.

I shove my spoon into the cold mush and begrudgingly take a bite. I chew the potatoes at the same speed as I am crawling along this trail.

The moon is glowing huge over the butte we just crested. We are in a burn zone, and everything that surrounds us has been stripped down by wildfire. The trees are charred sticks and the trail is soft dust. This forest is a barren wasteland. It looks as ravaged as I feel.

I push myself off the log and start to shuffle down the trail again. I look at my watch every seven steps and detest how resistant it is to forward progress. Time and distance can't *actually* be moving this slowly, I think. But my watch keeps assuring me that they are. I am stuck in a time warp, where everything has been reduced to the speed of glacial drip. As hard as I try, I can't make it go by any faster.

The trail descends into the matchstick trees. The downhill taunts me with how slow my pace remains. Surely, I should be able to move faster than this when I've got the force of the earth's core pulling me along. But I'm unable to shift into any gear that's quicker than a death march.

I search the dark night for any signs of the trailhead. Looking through the trees for a wide, boxy sign. I keep thinking I see it. But it's never really there. I am hallucinating signs around every bend in the trail.

There is a pack of wolves that roams this part of Oregon and I keep scanning the burn for their eyes, glowing as bright as the moon. I think about myself after my mother's diagnosis—the wolf caged alone with red-hot grief, with no escape.

I'm back in that cage now, clawing for a way out.

When my watch hits seventy miles, I want to celebrate. I have to be close. I don't think about the fact that watch mileage and map mileage are often misaligned.

"We must be almost there," I say to Ian. I'm desperate for good news.

"Do you want me to look at the map?" he asks.

"Yes, please." I am certain the map will tell us that we have less than a dozen steps to go.

Ian pulls out his phone and pulls up Gaia, which uses satellites to find us and show our location on the trail.

He uses his fingers to measure the distance. This is a terrible no good very bad sign. He wouldn't need to measure the distance if it was .01 miles, which is about the only mileage I can bear in this moment.

"Looks like we have about two miles left," he reports.

I collapse on a log. He might as well have said, "There is a firing squad ready for you."

February 2020

Eugene, Oregon

A few weeks after I got back from saying my final goodbye to my mom, I noticed that my dog Brutus's mouth was swollen and he wasn't acting like his typical rascal self. Even in his old age of thirteen and a half, he still scampered around the house with his tail nubbin wagging. He'd follow me into the kitchen, where he'd sit at my feet and look at me with his black saucer eyes, letting me know he was a good boy who was most deserving of a treat. He excitedly jumped into bed every night—where he'd circle the navy comforter seven times before body slamming my legs with all forty of his pounds to maximize his snuggle position.

When I noticed his jaw was a little puffy, I brought him to our vet, figuring it was a simple infection and a round of antibiotics would knock it out of him and get him back to good health.

I watched the vet pry his mouth open and shine her flashlight into it. She squinted her eyes and stared into the light's glow for a minute. She put the flashlight down and let Brutus jump off the table. He trotted back over to me and dug his snout into my lap and burrowed his face into my thigh. I put my hand on his scraggly black head and kneaded my fingers behind his ears. Brutus had been my greatest comfort through the grief of cancer, his body against mine was a deep breath and a hug. Every time my mom called me with bad news, she'd make sure Brutus was close by.

I looked up at the vet, expectantly waiting for the news of an infection.

"He's got a mass on the roof of his mouth," she said. She crossed her arms and gave Brutus a sad look. "We can do a biopsy if you want, but I believe it's malignant oral melanoma—a cancerous growth."

I was on the brink of a Category 5 meltdown. The grief from my mother's death still boiled inside me. It was scalding hot and churning at the tip of my throat. I didn't trust myself to respond without spilling it all out in the sterile vet office.

I just stared back at her. My eyes wide and terrified. Glassy with the tears that were ramming the floodgate behind them.

"Unfortunately, it's not treatable and it's usually fast-growing and life-ending. At this point, the best we can do is provide comfort care to Brutus and keep his quality of life as high as possible. But it's probably only a matter of weeks."

I bit my lip. Trying to use physical pain to squash the emotions that were about to erupt. Brutus nuzzled his nose deeper into my legs. I couldn't hide anything from him. Whenever I was on the phone with my mom or brother upstairs in my bedroom, I'd hear Brutus tiptoe over to the bottom of the stairs, where he'd wait and listen. I'd sniffle, quick and quiet. He'd hear the whisper of a sign that I was upset and come bounding up the stairs to burrow his face into my lap.

We left the vet's office and got in the car. I finally crumbled on the drive home. The sobs rolled through me like breaking waves. I got home and walked inside with Brutus tucked by my side. I collapsed in bed and he jumped next me, pressing his snout into my armpit to comfort me, just like he always did when I cried.

I hoped he didn't realize that this time I was crying over him.

When I got back from saying goodbye to my mom in Vermont, I didn't think I could handle another ounce of grief. I was on the edge of a cliff and a mouse's exhale could've pushed me off.

But as soon as the vet put her flashlight down and told me what she'd seen, I had to take a chisel to my broken heart and clear room for even more grief.

It didn't make sense to me that the world could work this way. That it could be so ruthless—Jess and my mother being diagnosed with cancer just weeks apart. Their diseases worsening on the same rapid and cruel trajectory. How my brother would pinball between hospital floors to see his dying mother and his sick wife. That before I'd even caught my breath from burying my mother, I could be counting down final exhales again.

Mile 132,
Crater Lake National Park

I spy the shadows of a trail sign poking through the dark forest. I don't know if it's a hallucination or real.

"Do you see that?" Ian asks, with a burst of excitement. Ian's tone is the answer I've been wanting for hours.

It is 2:30 A.M. I have been running for twenty straight hours. I stumble down the dark trail and collapse against the sign. My hands press into the cold wood, and I'm not sure I could stay upright without it.

The parking area is small and quiet. No one is there but our three vans parked together.

Nicole and Tom open their van door. Danielle and Jameson are asleep. Tom comes over and in a hushed voice tells me he's going to start grilling me a burger. Nicole and Tom offered to make me dinner at whatever obscene hour I finished. And their generosity is not deterred by the fact that it's 2:30 A.M.

I hear the Coleman stove creak open. The flick of a lighter and the fast whoosh of the burner igniting. A pan on the metal burner. The sizzle of meat cooking. I let the sounds settle over me, thinking about how this has been the soundtrack of my day, my friends offering unflinching support while I waded through my lowest lows. It's the same lullaby that's comforted me through loss, the friends who held space for my grief, as uncomfortable as it may be, to sit with deep sorrow.

I crawl into the bed and let the full weight of my body melt into the mattress. The two inches of memory foam that's been the subject of my fantasies for the last seventy-two miles.

I should take off my running clothes and put on dry sweats. But that feels like a Herculean task. So, I end the day just like I started it. Lying in bed, trapped beneath overwhelm.

I do not feel grateful to be done with my day. I do not feel proud of running seventy-two miles. Or of getting through the first two days as scheduled.

I just feel defeated by the day and by the mental low that I couldn't dig myself out of. I look up at the black sky through the window of the van. The stars glowing with the light I can't feel.

Positivity is on another planet.

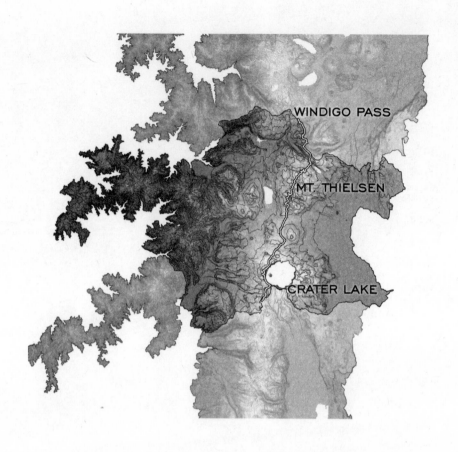

Three

POSSIBILITY IS A NORTH STAR

AUGUST 3, 2020
DAY THREE—CRATER LAKE NATIONAL PARK TO WINDIGO PASS
59.5 MILES, 6,745 FEET OF CLIMBING

Mile 133,
Crater Lake National Park

I can't face what's waiting for me on the other side of the van door.

I hear Ian's voice and then Danielle's talking outside. My crew is milling about the trailhead while I'm still hiding beneath my sleeping bag. They know it's not a good scene in here—or in my head. They watched me stumble into the dark campsite and collapse into bed. So tired I could barely peel the shoes off my feet or chew the burger they lovingly grilled in the middle of the night.

I don't want to step outside and have to talk about how I feel—physically or emotionally.

But more than I don't want to see anyone or let anyone see me, I have to pee.

I try to will my body to move itself out of this bed. But I have reached a level of exhaustion that leaves me with trust issues with my body, and I'm not sure I am capable of getting myself into an upright position.

I thrust one limb over the side of the bed and shift my weight onto my foot, and then shove the other one down to meet it. I brace myself against the bed and try to stand up.

Crap.

My legs quake beneath me. My limbs feel as stable as a broken stool trying to hold up an elephant. I'm not sure I can get myself out of this van, never mind run fifty-eight miles today.

"You can do this, Emily," I whisper to my legs in the most encouraging tone I can muster. Trying not to dwell on the fact that I have to give myself a pep talk to get out of a parked car.

My entire crew is outside the van when I stumble out of it. Nicole and Tom, Danielle and Jameson, Ian and the dogs. They all look at me in silence when I crack the door open. It feels like I just walked into a group where everyone has been talking about me behind my back.

My five-month-old puppy, Dilly, and Danielle's dog, Petra, bolt into the woods. I watch them effortlessly sprint around, hurdling downed trees and knee-high shrubs. I'm envious of their speed and agility and wish that one of them could tag in for me today. A designated hitter for my next fifty-eight miles.

"Good morning, friend!" Danielle sings. She's wearing a black puffy jacket and gray sweats. Stray hairs fly out from her brown ponytail.

I try to fake a smile. But I'm not sure my facial muscles are any more responsive than my lower extremities.

"Good morning," I say, trying to force some cheer into my greeting. "Excuse me for a second. I really have to pee."

My friends nod and mumble in response. I shuffle away, one awkward step at a time—while praying to a god I don't believe in that I look better than I feel. But that seems highly unlikely. Each leg is as stiff as a two-by-four, and I'm moving with the grace of a baby giraffe trying to walk for the first time.

Please don't watch me, I think. I need some human here to believe that I still have any chance of being able to do this—and I'm certainly not that person right now.

I imagine what my friends are thinking as they watch me walk into the woods: *Who does this girl think she is, trying to break a speed record? She can barely pop a squat and it's only her third day.*

My eyes well up with tears. I want to crumple to the ground, melt into the dirt, and disappear from this horrible moment and this silly goal forever.

Dilly and Petra whiz by me and I brace myself for canine impact. My muscles seize at the sudden movement. I don't think I could withstand a collision from my thirty-two-pound puppy right now.

They bolt deeper into the sparse forest, and I look for a tree that's wide enough to conceal at least a little bit of me. I left most of my already slim modesty back in Eugene, and I'm not worried about revealing a butt cheek or two. But I am concerned about how my body will handle a squat—and my crew watching it all unfold—or not fold at all.

I yank my sweats down and bend my knees to lower my body toward the earth.

My legs resist the bend. My quadriceps feel like overstretched rubber bands that will snap if I keep going. I feel like I need to submerge my legs into a hot tub for at least forty-eight hours straight before they will soften enough to fold.

I touch the ground to steady myself. My fingers grind into the dirt and quiver against the earth. The act of holding myself up to pee is so fatiguing that it rattles all the way into my hands.

The sky is bright blue overhead. The shadows of the trees are shrinking back into their trunks. A reminder of my late night and late start. I'll be running well into the night again—if I can get myself to start running at all.

I stumble back to my friends and say nothing when I see them. But my silence says everything that I can't bear to utter.

They scatter to give me space. I sit on the side of the van and collapse my face into my palms, elbows digging into my knees.

"Coffee?" Ian asks, as if the entire run isn't in question.

"I guess so," I sigh.

I see Danielle creeping over. Her tentative steps ask for consent to continue.

"Hiiii," I say, granting her permission to join me.

"Do you need a pep talk?" she asks. She wastes no time on pleasantries.

"Please, yes."

She looks at me. My face flushes red with shame. Her brown eyes soften with compassion.

She's been here before, I remind myself. Maybe this is exactly how she felt, too.

"Day two is a bear," she begins. "A mean, angry, vicious grizzly bear. Day two is so big and so hard. I don't think it's possible to finish day two feeling anything but assaulted by a violent carnivore."

She puts her hand on my shoulder and gives me a tight squeeze.

I rub a small tear out of the corner of my eye and laugh.

"I definitely feel like a bear beat me up and stole my lunch money," I say.

"Of course you do," Danielle says. "But you did it!"

She touches my arm and locks eyes with me. "You got through it. You ran every single one of those miles yesterday."

"I most definitely did not *run* every single one of those miles," I snap back. I picture the slow shuffle through the middle of the night—when each tenth of a mile felt like it took an entire fortnight to cover.

Danielle swats me. "You know what I mean! You finished every single mile. I don't care if you were crab walking by the end. You did it. You're here."

I nod. She is right. I did get through it. That had to be the hardest day of running of my life and I finished it.

"So, you can do it again today," she says. "That same badass woman who got through yesterday can get through another day today. And trust me, Emily. It is going to feel easier. You are going to surprise yourself with how strong you feel once you get going. Your body is adapting to the demands of this run, even if it doesn't feel like it yet."

I hear the sincerity in her voice, and it makes me want to believe her. She sounds so confident in me. *Can I feel some of that myself?*

Ian walks over holding a mug of steaming coffee. I take it from him and sip it, starting to paw through my duffel bag of gear. I'm not convinced I can actually get through the miles today, but I know I can't wave my white flag just yet. The idea of running fifty-eight miles still feels outrageous, but I'm not sure what else to do but get ready to run.

"What food do you want in your vest?" he asks. He starts sorting through my food bin and pulling out different options. He holds up a bag of Skittles. I nod. Then scowl at oatmeal cookies. Another nod for sour watermelon gummies. An "absolutely not" to a granola bar. I'm quickly learning which foods will be palatable out here and which are so revolting that I never want to see, smell, or chew them again.

He fills my bladder with water and shoves it into my hydration vest, handing me the pack that's now fat with gear.

The only thing that isn't ready is me.

I force myself to change into running clothes, peeling off my sweats and contorting each limb to slide into my standard trail uniform of split shorts, sports bra, and tank. I braid my long brown hair to one side and cover my head with my bright pink backward hat, stamped with a pickle graphic. It's my way to bring Dilly, whose full name is Dilly Pickle Chip, with me on this run while he's still too young to actually join me. I yank my socks and shoes onto my feet—which are already swollen with miles.

I let out a deep exhale and limp over to the trailhead. I force a grin for my crew as I walk away from them.

"Okay, here we go!" I squeak. I whack my poles together to compensate for the noise I can't summon up myself.

My friends cheer for me as I wobble away, their voices teeming with the support they know I need.

I look out at the trail. The thin strip of dirt disappears into the distance and stretches all the way to Washington. I don't know if I can get through a single mile today—never mind fifty-eight of them—never mind all the way to the other side of Oregon.

I think about how to muster up any belief that I still have a chance. I imagine turning my body upside down and shaking it until an ounce of hope falls out—like emptying a purse for the quarter you need to pass the tollbooth. Can I find something buried deep within me, even when it feels like all hope has been squashed?

June 2019
Oregon and Vermont

On the last day of chemotherapy, my mom got to ring a bell.

It's a tradition meant to commemorate the end of this critical phase of cancer treatment. Chemotherapy gets a coveted checkmark on the "fight cancer" to-do list—and that's something worth celebrating after it's upended your life with months of treatments and a biweekly cocktail of toxins.

She sent me a video afterward. She sat in the same chair she'd visited six times over the course of four months. A fleece blanket over her lap. A colorful beanie on her bald head. I looked closer. It was covered in daisies, a hopeful nod to brighter seasons ahead.

She reached up to the bell and grabbed ahold of it. Her arm swung back and forth with relief. A smile flooded her face. She laughed as it chimed. The nurses cheered her on in the background.

I watched it from beneath my comforter in Oregon and wept. I replayed it for Ian and cried again.

My mom had endured months of chemotherapy and its ruthless side effects. The nausea, the fatigue, the hair loss, the constant injections, the days and weeks of feeling like a stranger in her own body. The fear of cancer's wrath stewing inside her.

And now she was done with it. The bell, the period at the end of this long sentence.

I watched it again and let out a deep sigh. I felt like I'd been holding my breath for months. And watching her ring that bell was permission to exhale.

I could finally think about my mom getting better.

A few weeks later, she had a follow-up appointment with her oncologist to go over her scans. I asked to listen in from Oregon.

She put me on speaker and set the phone down on Dr. Jackson's desk. I heard her say that I was on the line. Her doctor may have nodded, but no time was wasted on greetings. She plunged straight into the update.

"There's still cancer," she said. There was no sugarcoating anything. Her voice was somber and apologetic.

My heart sank all the way to my toes. I felt my insides hollow. *There was still cancer after twelve rounds of chemotherapy?* I hadn't even realized this was a possibility.

Of course, it was a possibility. But not one that I had entertained. I believed my mother would get rid of the cancer and then we would worry about it coming back. I hadn't realized that the first step might never happen. She rang the bell.

"We have limited ways to keep treating you here," her oncologist went on. My mother had a rare cancer—one that had few treatment options after that first round of chemotherapy.

"We can look into clinical trials at Dana-Farber and see if you're a candidate for anything there.

"Or we can treat you through radiation here, but it will not be to cure it, it will be to manage it," she went on.

The conversation ended and my mom promised she'd call me later as she walked out of Dr. Jackson's office. A door closed in the background and echoed down a stairwell. I could hear her voice crack as she said goodbye. She might not ever say it out loud to me, but I knew that she was as scared as I was.

The next day I got in my car and drove to the mountains. I'd spent the entire night curled up in a ball in my bed, with Brutus tucked beside me. I knew I needed to force myself out of the house—I knew I needed to move through the fear and anxiety.

My mother's cancer had scared me from that first phone call, but "there's still cancer" turned the disease into an imminent threat. A finger hovering over the trigger.

My hands clenched the steering wheel and my eyes locked on the hot asphalt. The sky was a bright blue; the sun beamed high above. Thick Douglas firs towered over the road. The vibrant summer day was a stark contrast to everything I felt inside. Inside me was the darkest fear, spilling through my blood like black oil. Inside me was my mother's death.

I kept driving up the mountain pass. I got out of the car and ran around a lake that's so big, it disappears into the horizon on every shoreline. I ran until my lungs and legs burned with fatigue. I ran until my breaths were as frantic as my fears. I ran until I was back at my car hours later, where I collapsed against the side of it and started to sob. I could run around this lake until I couldn't walk anymore. But I couldn't outrun the reality that my mother might die.

I booked a flight back to Vermont for the next week. I hadn't been back since my mom's initial surgery in January because she kept telling me to wait.

"Visit when I feel better," she'd say.

But she didn't resist this time. We both knew she might never feel better again.

I landed in Vermont on a hot July day. I watched the familiar landscape draw closer as the plane descended. The rolling farmland and the meandering contours of Lake Champlain stretched out below. The bird's-eye view of Vermont usually lulled me into warm nostalgia. But today, I was numb to everything.

I got off the plane and waded through the busy airport. People rushed by with carry-ons over their shoulders, coffees in hand. Flight announcements bellowed through loudspeakers. I marched through it in a daze, oblivious to the buzz around me. As I got closer to the sliding glass doors, I saw her.

My mom was waiting for me on the other side. She always waited for me in the terminal. No matter what time of day I landed. Fresh off a red-eye or pushing midnight. She would get there early, with enough time to find parking and get inside, so that she was always the first thing I saw when I stepped through those doors. Coming home to Vermont was coming home to my mom.

She was exactly where I knew she would be. Shifting her weight from foot to foot. She was wearing a loose black shirt and khaki capris, paired with her purple Keen sandals. Even after retirement, she always dressed like an elementary schoolteacher. Her head was still bald from the chemotherapy; her small glasses rested on her face. Her eyes searched through the crowd, widening with excitement when they landed on me.

I felt another gut-punch of dread when I spotted her. I couldn't look at her in the flesh without seeing the shadow of death right behind her.

She bounced up and down on her toes as I got closer. Lifting and lowering her heels with anticipation. She drew me in for a hug the second I walked through the door. I swallowed back tears. I didn't want her to know how scared I was. I didn't want her to feel how close her death sat in my head.

"I'm so glad you're here," she sighed. She stayed tight at my side as we walked out of the airport and into the hot summer outside. She slipped her arm through mine, leaned her head onto my shoulder and gave me another tight squeeze.

We drove straight to the shore of Lake Champlain, where a paved bike path meanders along the lake for miles.

It was the same path where I cheered her into the finish of her first marathon. When I lost my voice from cheering so hard and my index finger blistered from ringing a cowbell every time I saw her.

It was also where we'd finished one of our many races together. A photographer caught us during one of the miles along the waterfront. When my mom saw him aiming his camera in our direction, she slung her arm around my shoulder in a running hug and her smile stretched as wide as the lake behind us.

We'd been on countless runs together on the bike path, and it was the obvious place to go immediately after I landed, especially since she was feeling good enough to get out and do something.

She changed into her bike gear in the driver's seat and I slid on my running clothes. She pulled her bike off the rack on the back of her bright red Nissan SUV.

"I rode twenty miles last week," she told me, beaming. The break from chemotherapy had given her more energy and she'd seized it to get out. She'd been biking, walking longer distances, and traveling around New England with her girlfriends.

"You're amazing," I said, with an impressed sigh. I thought about how I'd had to force myself to run after that call with her oncologist. She got in the car the next day and drove to Maine with her friend Heather. She sent me photos of lobster rolls, lighthouses, and sunset cruises, smiling in every single one. I'd scrolled through them from the fetal position on my bedroom floor.

We walked to the path together and then she hopped on her bike.

"See you in a few miles!" she called, as she bounced away with excited pedal strokes.

I watched her disappear into the distance as I ran, clinging onto the sight of her until she was gone. I kept running after her, surrounded by hot asphalt and dry grass.

I ran along the lake. My feet slapped against the pavement. My skin was clammy with sweat from the humid Vermont air. My breaths were quick and shallow. But just like that day in Oregon, I couldn't outrun the reality of why I was there.

I tried to shake that thought out of my head. But my fears hung with me every step. *The chemotherapy didn't work. Her options were running out. The cancer was still there. The cancer was growing. My mom was dying.*

The familiar landscape was a blur around me. I was oblivious to everything but my pulsing anxiety—every brain cell fixated on the worst thing that could happen. We were on the bike path together because we might never have the chance to do this again.

I heard her catch up with me before I saw her. I'd reached my halfway point and started running back to the car.

"Emily!" she cried. I turned and saw her gliding toward me, a huge grin stretched across her face.

She slowed her pedal stroke as she got closer and pulled up next to me.

"I just love riding along the lake," she said with a sigh. "Look at the Adirondacks today."

I looked to my right. Waves of blue mountains rose up beyond the far shore of Lake Champlain. I'd been staring at the mountains across the lake for almost two hours and hadn't even registered them.

We finished the last mile back to the car together. I sprinted after her bike while she pedaled ahead.

She kept chattering as fast as my feet hit the pavement.

"Should we get maple creemees or cookies when we're done?" she asked. "Or both? We should definitely get both."

I watched her ride in front of me. She was so happy to be out there. On a bike. Along the lake. With her daughter running behind her.

It wasn't an act that she was forcing for me; she was sincerely brimming with joy.

I knew she was scared. We'd gotten the same horrible news on that call with her doctor—and it was her life on the line. I heard her voice crack with fear after her oncologist told her the cancer was still there. But she wasn't curling into the fetal position on her bedroom floor. She was biking along Lake Champlain with her daughter running behind her, talking about where to get maple creemees after the ride.

I couldn't think about anything other than how scared I was that she was dying—but she was still focused on how to keep living.

Mile 138,
Crater Lake National Park

Sunlight spills through the ferns as I start running. I am alone with the sound of my feet on the dirt and the memories of my mom on the bike path.

My legs loosen up as I pad down the flat stretch of trail. It somehow feels easier to run this mile than it did to squat to pee just an hour ago.

It still feels impossible that I could run fifty-eight miles today, but I try to not dwell on it. I push that thought out of my head and let myself feel good for at least this moment, for at least this step. On a day when I thought the first step might never happen, I've already surpassed my expectations for myself by simply starting—and maybe I can keep doing that if I don't talk myself out of this run.

I remember doing my first 100-miler seven years ago, through Oregon's Siskiyou Mountains. After I finished, people asked me how I did it. How I kept running for twenty-seven hours, straight through the night, up and over mountain after mountain. And the most honest thing I could tell them was that I had an unwavering belief that I would get to the finish line. And when my quadriceps turned to chopped hamburger meat and blisters ate at my feet, and hallucinations turned every stone into a coiled rattlesnake, I kept returning to the same thought: I could finish the race. I would finish the race. And I did.

I run through an open meadow. Crisp dry grass rises up beside me. The trail spikes uphill and I follow it, slowing my gait to a hike. I push my poles into the earth to help me up the climb.

I crest the hill and see Crater Lake flood the horizon. Its shade is almost too blue to believe. Wizard Island floats majestically in the middle of the deep sapphire water. Craggy mountains tower over the lakeshore.

My mom and I always talked about coming here together. I know she would've loved it. She gravitated toward dramatic coastlines and lakes straight off a postcard. When she visited me in Oregon for the first time, we drove the hour out to the coast and stopped at an overlook perched above a lighthouse. She gawked at the white tower, nestled into a sweeping cliffside, with childlike wonderment.

A pang of regret hits me. That I never brought her here and got to see her light up with awe. That the chance to share this lake with my mom is gone forever.

There are so many moments of grief like this—where the reality of her death whittles an even deeper hole inside me. There are so many ways I keep losing my mother.

On the other side of the hill, I see my crew vans in the distance—Jameson's polished sprinter next to Ian's janky blue van. I run toward them—and see my crew bouncing up and down. Their exuberance is undoubtedly fueled by surprise that I made it more than a few steps.

"What can we get for you?" Ian asks and gives me a hug, braving the dirt and sweat that cover my body.

It's a quick pit stop. Water bladder topped off, a few bites of a strawberry Pop-Tart, and I'm back on my way. Ian runs beside me along the shoreline, which drops hundreds of feet down to the glimmering water below.

"You're doing great!" he says, sounding much more sincere than he did this morning. He's clearly shocked to see me running—and running quite well.

"I actually feel pretty good," I tell him, as we weave through the crowds of tourists. I'm as surprised as he is that I'm moving as well as I am.

We run up and down the small hills that overlook the lake and I savor the views as we go. Each pitch is short and steep. A grind of a hike followed by a quick tumble downhill. And then the PCT peels off into a meadow that will carry me away from the buzz of the crowds and the deep blue water. I pivot my head to take in one more glimpse of the lake. It's easy to see my mom, standing at the edge, eyes wide and alive. I hold onto that image as I keep running.

I run through the vast landscape under a hot midday sun, my stride flowing with the miles, until I see the crew vans again. I've now covered eighteen miles and it's time for a longer stop.

As I stumble into the dirt parking area, Danielle pulls out a camp chair and tells me to sit down.

"Let's change your socks and shoes," she says. Her words are fast and commanding. It's an order, not a suggestion.

She pulls off my socks, which are crusty with sweat and dirt, and gives my feet a quick check for hot spots.

Jameson is ready to go—looking as impeccably prepared as always. Her hair is pulled back in tight braids. Her clothes look brand-new next to my sweaty and dusty gear. Her laces are double-knotted. She'll run the next twenty miles with me, until Danielle runs me through the final twenty-two miles of the day—into the middle of the night.

I take bites of hot quesadillas, sipping on cold Coke between bites. The salty, greasy food tastes better than anything I have in my pack.

I lace up my shoes and we take off, into the hot and dry woods, heading north toward the rocky spires of Mount Thielsen—and the state of Washington. I've already gone farther than I thought I could this morning—and as I clip off the next mile, I wonder how much farther I can go.

August 2019

My mom didn't hesitate to pursue the clinical trial route. If there was any chance she could still rid her body of cancer, she was going to take it.

But to participate in a clinical trial isn't as easy as just signing up. There were mandatory tests and panels of doctors to clear. She was disqualified from one trial because she didn't have quite enough cancerous cells in her body—which was wild to think back on, when just a few months later, her cancer had exploded so aggressively that she was transitioned to hospice. Each rejection sent me into a new spiral of hopelessness, each one thrust her into a deeper state of determination.

Most of the trials she considered weren't designed for her exact cancer, because it was so rare, but they were deemed similar enough to try. She finally was admitted to a trial for a different kind of uterine cancer because she checked enough of the right boxes. On the day she found out she was in, you'd have believed she was deemed cancer-free. Our family celebrated the news from Oregon to Vermont—and the glimmer of hope it offered.

She started traveling to Boston from Vermont every two weeks—driving four hours in each direction. Her appointments involved hours of injections, along with tests and checkups with her medical team. The trial quickly became something that required an overnight stay.

She approached each trip to Dana-Farber as she had her first walks after surgery. She recruited friends and family to join her and found ways to make each day in Boston about something other than just cancer. A walk along a portion of the Boston Marathon course, glazed donuts at a new bakery, strolls through urban gardens. Her cousin brought Cape Cod Chips with sea salt for the long drive. "Because I like the ocean," she said.

I clamored for updates from her medical team, dissecting each bit of information for clues about her chances of survival. I scoured the internet for research papers, as if I'd find proof that she'd be okay on the twelfth page of Google results, or buried deep in the footnotes from a decades-old publication. I pored over data from her scans, as if I could save my mom if I just looked hard enough. I channeled my powerlessness into a desperate hunt for answers, and I couldn't rest until I found evidence that my mom would live.

She didn't talk about what would happen if the clinical trial didn't work. She snapped a picture of a rock in an atrium at Dana-Farber and sent it to me, the word *hope* etched on the smooth stone.

Mile 160,
Mount Thielsen Wilderness

We crest the shoulder of Mount Thielsen. The summit of the mountain is a towering spire surrounded by sharp cliffs, the "lightning rod of the Cascades." I can see Diamond Peak on the horizon, the next major mountain that I'll run to, if I can make it through today and start tomorrow. I turn around and see the peaks that surround Crater Lake. They already look far away. I lift my arm up and scrunch two fingers together to frame the mountains. They're just a couple of inches high.

I did that, I think. *I covered that distance with my own two legs today. The same legs that could barely get out of a van this morning ran all the way from there to here.* I look ahead again, at the wide summit of Diamond Peak and the ripples of mountains beyond it. I imagine myself running past each one, my legs turning the insurmountable distance into inches on the horizon behind me, carrying me farther than I ever believed possible.

Summer 2013
Vermont

My mom decided to attempt her first triathlon the year she turned sixty. It was an especially impressive goal because while she could stay afloat, she didn't really know how to swim. At least not in a way that would get her through a triathlon, where she would need to travel about half a mile through open water.

She learned how to do freestyle, or front crawl, and started visiting her local pool through the dead of winter to practice. She'd scrape the ice off her car and drive to the gym while the temperature hovered below zero degrees. At a time of year when swimming was probably one of the least appealing forms of exercise to most Vermonters because the preferred apparel was seven layers of fleece and down, she kept diligently doing her laps.

"I've decided that when I swim, I have a job to do," she said, "and that job is to make everyone else in the pool look good."

She could only complete one lap of freestyle when she started, but she gradually worked her way up past thirty—more than the distance she'd need to cover in her first race.

She finished that first sprint triathlon, where she swam a half mile in a lake, biked over twelve miles, and ran a 5k, but she was still uneasy in the water. During one of her early races, she looked down at the weedy lake beneath her while she was swimming and started to hyperventilate. She emerged rattled and in last place. Nevertheless, she finished that race and insisted that she wanted to do another.

"I don't want my fear of open water to keep me away from triathlons," she said.

She signed up for another race and before the start, she went to the shore and stared out at the lake. I don't know if she felt determination or intimidation when she gazed out at the glassy water—or both. But I know that when the race started, she jogged into the lake and plunged in. She took it one buoy at a time. She told me that she counted strokes and sang in her head. She turned over and did sidestroke when she needed to take a deep breath. She made it back to the shore and walked out onto the beach, lake water dripping off her slick wetsuit and bright green swim cap. She finished the race and said she was ready for the next one.

She was like that with all her goals. Her first marathon. Her triathlon. Her solo travels. Her skydiving. Her half marathon PRs, which is runner shorthand for "personal records," a phrase that we use to talk about our best times.

I'm sure she had doubts and fears about everything, just as she'd had with swimming, but she didn't dwell on them—and she certainly didn't let them stop her.

She wasn't deterred by how hard it would be to learn how to swim as an adult. She didn't swear off triathlons after she had that panic attack in the water. I don't remember her ever sharing that she might not finish her first marathon. She just kept going, with her determined gaze and soft smile.

That's what I remember most about my mom and every goal that she ever chased. That's what I'll always remember about the way she lived with cancer. That hope and possibility prevailed over any doubt or fear that she may have felt. That even when she was slapped with the most dismal setback, or slim odds, or defeating news, she held onto hope. She found a reason to take the next step.

Mile 191,
Umpqua National Forest

The sky is black and all I can see are the silhouettes of trees and the beam of my headlamp on the trail. Danielle and I are nearing the end of the day that didn't seem possible fifty-seven miles ago. It's almost midnight, when every mile feels longer and my eyelids grow heavier by the minute.

"We need a song!" says Danielle. She knows the power of a pop song when I'm struggling to keep my eyes open.

"Robyn," I say.

She fires up "Dancing On My Own" on her phone and the Swedish pop ballad floats into the quiet night. I throw my arms up in the air and pick up my pace. We bounce down the trail, two-stepping over rocks and roots as we go.

I think back to this morning, when I could barely squat to pee. I couldn't fathom running fifty-eight miles. It seemed impossible that I could cover any part of this day without motorized assistance. There were way more reasons to believe I should quit than to believe I could finish.

And now I'm dancing down the trail—with a full day of running behind me.

I think about when I was deciding to do this run. I hadn't run anything longer than 100 miles, not even a quarter of the mileage it would take to cross the state. But although I had very little evidence to back me up, I chose to believe I had a chance.

The clinical trial didn't work for my mom. The cancer exploded in her body in just a few months. It spread to new organs and resisted the drugs that were injected into her bloodstream. The disease festered and grew until it consumed so much of her that her death was imminent.

But in another life, in another body, it *could've* worked. Her hope and determination might've transformed into more miles on the bike path. Her hope for another day might've grown into decades.

Possibility was my mom's North Star. It kept her moving through her first marathon, through learning to swim as a sixty-year-old woman, through trying to survive cancer, so she could pedal into old age.

It might not have made any sense to start running this morning, when I could barely pee in the woods. When it seemed impossible to believe I could even cover a fraction of the day's distance.

But to not leave the trailhead, to not even try, would've meant taking a match to any chance of reaching the border—and watching it burn to ash. Stepping onto the trail this morning was a gesture of hope, even if it felt like I didn't have an ounce of it in me at the time.

I see the familiar shadows of cars parked up ahead. A rush of excitement hits when I see how close I am to the end of this day. As my feet move over the dusty trail and carry me closer to my stopping point, I think about all the doubts and fears that still stand between me and Washington. I made it through today, but I still have nearly 300 miles to go. I'm sure this morning will not be the last time that I feel defeat bearing down on me.

I take my last steps of the day thinking about my mom on the bike path, flying toward me with her bright eyes and soft smile, pedaling toward possibility, and I hold onto her like she held onto hope.

Four

THE CHARLTON LAKE PARTY

AUGUST 4, 2020
DAY FOUR—WINDIGO PASS TO CHARLTON LAKE
48.3 MILES, 6,401 FEET OF CLIMBING

Winter 2019
Eugene, Oregon

After my mom was diagnosed, laughter felt like a betrayal.

I remember sitting on my bed on a cold February afternoon, curled under a blue fleece blanket, when I got a text from her.

"Feeling terrible from chemotherapy," she said. "Trying to remember that it's doing its job and this needs to happen."

I pictured her in Vermont, staring out the four-paned windows in the living room, watching fat snowflakes fall outside. I wondered how many winters she had left.

Could this be her last one?

The thought pierced the most tender part of my heart. I choked as a fast sob rushed my throat.

Brutus jumped onto the bed and burrowed his nose into my armpit to comfort me. When I let another sob escape, he shimmied his butt into my side, as if the right spot would make everything better. A sniffle sent him mining my body for a more effective snuggle.

I looked up. He was digging his black, hairy rump into my abdomen, with all forty of his pounds propelling his efforts to burrow his way to a happier me.

I laughed. And then swallowed it back. How could I laugh in the same world where my mother was living with cancer? How could I laugh when my mother might be watching one of her last snowstorms?

There was nothing funny about that.

I felt like I needed to allow cancer to fill every crack and crevice of my world, like water finding every cranny of a tide pool. Because what else mattered when my mother was sick?

A friend texted later and asked if Eli and I wanted to join her at the climbing gym.

"What do you think?" Eli asked.

I looked back at him in silence. The obvious answer was to stay home. The idea of climbing across the bright rainbow-colored holds at the bouldering gym felt like a violation of the rules of cancer.

How could I be happy in the same world where my mom was dying? How could I play? How could I have fun, as if the clock wasn't ticking through my mother's final months, weeks, days, minutes, and breaths?

Joy and cancer could not coexist in my head.

Mile 210,
Diamond Peak Wilderness

I'm running on a sliver of trail that charges straight at Diamond Peak—and remembering how much I questioned my plan for today. I still think it might be an incredibly dumb decision.

I look up at Diamond Peak. It's the next volcano that I'll run by, easily distinguishable from the other Cascades because its summit stretches flat like a plateau, instead of a pointy peak like a child's drawing of a mountain. I once tried to get Diamond tattooed on my forearm, but the artist refused.

"It looks like a table," he said.

But up here, running through its highest meadows, it's hard to imagine how anyone could see this mountain as anything but a work of alpine art. Lingering snow clings to its rocky edges, rich evergreens dot the landscape, and an icy creek meanders through the lush

meadow—which is splattered with bright wildflowers, like a rainbow of
stars exploding across a night sky.

I'm running with my friend Daniel, who called dibs on pacing this
stretch of trail while the idea of this run was still a young fledgling. As
soon as I shared my plan to run across Oregon, Daniel piped in with a
quick, "I'll pace you past Diamond Peak!"

Diamond Peak is Eugene's backyard playground, and this wilderness
is cherished terrain for any trail runner, backpacker, or Douglas fir fan
in our community. Daniel grew up in Eugene and has been venturing
up here for hikes since he could waddle down the trail with a dinosaur
backpack full of snacks.

I haven't been coming here for quite as long. But I've been visiting
this area since I moved to Oregon seven years ago, at the age of twenty-
eight, after four years of living and working in Washington, DC, where
some of the closest wilderness was the manicured grass on the National
Mall. I was a brand-new trail runner when I moved to Oregon, and this
part of the state was the setting for many of my most formative outings:
my first solo overnight hike, with my heavy green backpack and a bor-
rowed sleeping bag, my first real alpine run, when we ran twenty-two
miles around one of the bluest lakes in the world and my eyes got wider
around every bend in the trail, and my first big solo trail runs, where I
built the confidence and skills to keep pushing myself in the backcountry.

When I was getting into trail running and outdoor adventures, I felt
like I needed to tag along with others because I didn't trust myself to go
alone. I thought if I tried to hack it solo, I'd end up lost and afraid and
eating poisonous mushrooms for sustenance. The mountains and forests
that surround Diamond Peak are where I learned how to navigate trails,
filter water, assess risks and conditions, and move my body confidently
and safely through the wilderness.

This stretch of the outdoors helped me progress from running my
first ultra in an urban park, to attempting to run across the entire state.
It feels right that I get to move through this place as I tackle the biggest

run of my life, especially after trudging through so much self-doubt over the last few days.

Waking up today felt different from every other morning on the trail, when I've been bombarded with overwhelm and defeat as soon as I blinked my eyes open. A question mark has punctuated my other days, but today, I know I can do it.

I only need to run forty-eight miles to reach Charlton Lake, where I'll stop for the night. I never thought I'd consider forty-eight miles an approachable distance, but now it almost feels like a sprint, after waking up to a seventy-mile monster day just two days ago. If I can be efficient, I could finish the mileage in daylight, which would be like Christmas in August.

When I was mapping out my plan, I found a compelling reason to do a shorter day today. I realized I could end the day at one of the closest spots on the PCT to Eugene—and I could arrange my schedule so that it fell on a Tuesday night, which is the night that my running group, fondly known as "the Hunt," has run together for over a decade.

Tuesday has been a sacred day for me since my first run with the group just a few weeks after I moved to Oregon. The ritual has become as dependable as the sun rising in the east. We run six to ten miles around South Eugene and then share beer and chips in my friend's basement, surrounded by portraits of Tom Selleck and tattered race bibs. We rotate leaders every week—sometimes the route is a straightforward loop of our local trails, and other times we're floating down the river with two-liter soda bottles as life rafts. When Ian and I started dating, it took him all of a week to learn that Tuesdays were booked and not a day we'd ever be hanging out, no matter how excited I was about our budding relationship.

When I realized I could reach one of the PCT's closest points to Eugene on a Tuesday night, I threw the idea out to the group. It would be like a Hunt field trip. Same night. Same ritual. Just a few miles up the road.

The idea was met with excited offers to pace, crew, and be at the lake with a healthy supply of beer and chips. The "hell yeses" rolled in one after another.

So, I penned it in. Saturday, August 1, would be my starting date. Tuesday night, I'd end up at Charlton Lake.

But as much as I loved the idea, I questioned my decision.

Isn't the point of this run to suffer as much as I can? To push myself into the deepest corner of the pain cave and see if I can keep running? Do serious athletes plan their competitive efforts around eating chips on a lake with friends? I thought about adding another five to ten miles to the day.

Building my run around a party on a lake didn't seem compatible with such a serious endeavor.

Winter 2019
Lincoln, Vermont

As soon as my mom could walk after her first surgery, she started a ritual that helped her keep putting one foot in front of the other.

When I arrived in Vermont after her hysterectomy, she was confined to the couch for her initial recovery, limited to traveling up and down the stairs just once a day. If she needed anything from her bedroom, I would fetch it for her.

But as she started to feel better, she could move around more—and she did. My childhood home is a two-story house, built around a red brick chimney and a tall black woodstove. The four downstairs rooms open into one another and she would walk circles around this configuration, counting her laps and diligently staying within her surgeon's recommendation for physical activity because she was a rule-follower and she wanted her recovery to be as smooth and swift as possible. She would share new milestones as she passed the woodstove. "Twelve laps today! I think I can do fifteen tomorrow."

On the fourth day I was home, she announced that she was ready for more.

"I'm going to walk up and down the driveway today," she said. Her blue eyes glowed. "Do you want to come with me?"

We walked down the driveway, our boots leaving a trail of footprints in the snow. And when we got to the quiet dirt road at the bottom, she gazed out at it.

"Tomorrow," she said. Her eyes danced.

She invited her cousin Mary to join us the next day. The three of us walked back down the driveway and turned onto the snow-covered road.

"I'm going to walk to the corner soon," my mom said. Her gaze charged into the distance.

By the end of my time in Vermont, we were walking to the corner, roughly a quarter mile from the front door.

She kept going every day after I left—and she started recruiting friends to join her. She posted an open invitation on social media, and people responded with eager offers to walk with her. She filled up her dance card with walking partners for the next month.

"I might have to start turning people away," she joked.

I got daily reports when I was back in Oregon about who she was walking with and where they went. Teacher friends on Monday. My dad's sister, Julie, and her golden retrievers on Tuesday. My brother and Jess, who was in the middle of her own treatment, and their dogs Jaxon and Willard on Wednesday.

"We went all the way to Briggs Hill today!" she texted, with a photo of her beaming alongside Jess and Jameson, fur hood pulled up tight over her face. Her smile radiated through the biting cold of the Vermont winter.

"These walks are the best part of every day," she said. "You should've seen the bright blue sky against the snow this morning."

When she started chemotherapy, she kept walking with friends every day, adjusting the distance when the fatigue was too much. Instead of filling every crack and crevice of her life with cancer, she made room for what gave her joy.

Mile 214,
Diamond Peak Wilderness

"Do you want me to recite one of Miles's books for you?" Daniel asks, as we hop over a creek. Daniel is the type of dad who will whip out his phone to show you the latest photos of his son before you've even said hello.

He doesn't wait for an answer before starting to prove that he can, in fact, recite his toddler's book *Giraffes Can't Dance* from memory.

"Gerald was a tall giraffe, whose neck was long and slim," he begins.

It's a stark contrast to yesterday, when I asked Danielle if she could play me a romance novel, because I knew she listened to them during her run across Oregon. I thought it was hilarious that her motivational fuel was raunchy reads instead of fast pop songs or pulsing hip-hop. When she confessed that she hadn't downloaded any books before the run, I requested that she make one up. And she proceeded to entertain me with a Danielle original tale about a mysterious hiker and the things he would do to her clitoris.

"The warthogs started waltzing, and the rhinos rock and rolled." Daniel is pages deep in the book.

I laugh and let him keep going. My thoughts drift back to a few miles ago, when I hit a huge milestone right after we skirted the crystal waters of Summit Lake. I'd been looking at my watch all morning in anticipation of reaching it. When I saw the digits flip, I stopped and shouted it out to the forest, my arms flew up, stretching to the sky with the evergreens that swallowed the trail.

"Two hundred miles!" I squealed. The excitement of covering 200 miles on foot rolled through me like champagne bubbles. Two hundred miles felt like possibility. Like I'm actually making my way to the other side of Oregon.

We're on the northern edge of Diamond Peak when we spy a colorful commotion ahead. A blur of fuchsia and cobalt jumps out through the thick trees. We haven't seen another soul all day, but now, loud cheers swell through the empty forest.

As we get closer, I see that it's my friends, Eric and Gretchen, with armfuls of food. They've hiked miles up the trail with their dog Fitz Roy to surprise me with trail magic, a widespread practice in the thru-hiking community, when hikers find an unexpected treat, or act of kindness, on the trail. Ice cream at a highway crossing, cubes of cold watermelon on the hottest summer day—or Dairy Queen in the middle of the Diamond Peak Wilderness, nearly halfway through a run across Oregon.

"Yay, Emily!" they cry as I bounce up to them. Gretchen is wearing a pink satin prom dress straight from 1987 and Eric is sporting a bright tropical shirt. They shove blue to-go boxes at me—filled with french fries and a hot dog. Followed by a Rice Krispie Treat and a Powerade that's still icy when I take a slug of it.

"We froze it so it would be cold when we gave it to you," Gretchen says.

"You guys are actual saints," I manage between gulps. The drink is as cold as glacial runoff and I'm ready to nominate them for MacArthur Genius awards for their brilliant move.

Fitz jumps up to shower me in kisses. His fluffy black tail wags at a rate of a million swings a minute. I take a bite of the hot dog—and squeal. It's one of the best things I've eaten all week. The Powerade is liquid gold. If I had a tail myself, I'd be wagging it even harder than Fitz right now.

"I actually want to eat all of this!" I moan as I bite into another french fry. I relish the feeling of hundreds of calories jetting into my bloodstream. "Trail magic, indeed."

"You look so good!" Eric says, and I can tell he means it.

I savor bites of food while telling them about the last few days. I'll see them again tomorrow night at our campsite on McKenzie Pass, before Eric paces me through one of my biggest days on the trail.

"We're so proud of you, Emily," Gretchen says.

"Thank you so, so much for this," I say, knowing I can't adequately express my gratitude for their kindness. I scratch Fitz's ears one more time, running his soft fur between my fingers. "I could hang out with you and your magical Powerade for hours."

I turn to Daniel.

"Are you ready?" I ask him.

"Let's go!" he yells and claps his hands together.

Eric and Gretchen cheer us on as we jog away. Their voices stay with me well after they fade from earshot.

February 2019
Santiam Pass, Oregon

My friend Nate asked me to go skiing a couple of weeks after I got back from Vermont. My initial instinct was to politely decline the invitation. Skiing felt like the bright holds of the bouldering gym. It wasn't a place that I could go in the same world where my mother was sick.

But I thought about my mom, choosing to get out every day to do something she loved—and I opened up the closet where I stored my ski gear.

"I'm in," I texted Nate.

We met before dawn the next morning and drove up to the mountains together. I struggled to make conversation on the drive, as my thoughts kept getting yanked away by my mom and cancer.

By the time we were at the trailhead, the sun was up and soft wisps of clouds hung in the sky.

I grabbed my skis from the back of Nate's car and mindlessly went through the motions of getting ready. I pulled my skins over the bottoms of my skis to give me traction so my skis could hike uphill on snow.

I zipped my fleece up to my chin as we started climbing through the crisp morning. I let Nate pull ahead and settled into the rhythm of sliding one ski in front of the other. I watched the lilac planks of my skis cut through the snow. The sun floated higher above us. I looked up at the sky.

The high alpine sky is the brightest blue I know. It's almost too blue to believe, like the shade of an ice-cold Powerade. The sky popped against the white landscape below.

I thought about my mom, walking down the dirt road that meanders past big red barns and cow pastures to reach her white house on the hill. It was easy to picture her looking up at the sky over the snowy hills of Vermont—and marveling at how bright it was on a clear winter day.

I inhaled the blue sky, the mountain air, the lullaby of moving my body through the wilderness. My heart rate jumped as I hiked, but my soul felt more settled than it had in weeks. The heaviness of cancer still weighed on me, but being in the mountains made it easier to take the next step.

Mile 219,
Diamond Peak Wilderness

As we keep running toward the highway, I feel like this day is the Benjamin Button of mileage. I'm gaining energy as I go, instead of losing it to all the miles I've covered. My stride is propelled by trail magic, warm memories, beloved wilderness, and the promise of what's ahead.

We pass a chain of turquoise lakes, tucked into evergreen groves. I remember bringing Brutus to one of these lakes on the other side of Diamond Peak for a mile-long backpacking trip when he was an elderly schnauzer. We had the lake to ourselves, and it felt like we were buried in backcountry wilderness, even though we were just a few thousand steps from the trailhead. We ate cold pizza on a log, and Brutus scavenged sticks along the shore. We fell asleep snuggled in the tent, looking at constellations through the mesh ceiling.

I smile at the memory and feel myself dart a little faster down the trail.

We cover the last few miles to the road and cross the highway to get to the trailhead, where my friend Justin is waiting to take over pacing duties. Ian and Dilly are stretching out after a nap in the shade of the van.

Justin is a gear nerd and looks the part in his matching Salomon ensemble. He hands me a bag of nacho cheese puffs.

"I knew I couldn't show up without at least one bag of chips," he tells me.

I pop the bag open and grab a handful.

Ian walks over to me with fresh socks. I unlace my shoes and peel off my grimy pair. A bright red blister shines from my fourth toe.

"I think I need to pop this guy," I tell Ian. He grabs a lighter and plunges a needle into the flame to sanitize it. He pokes the blackened tip into the swollen blister.

"Lanced!" he announces. I tape up the drained blister and pull new socks over my feet. The act of popping blisters on trail is controversial, since it can increase the risk of an infection. But I've decided I'll gladly accept that risk for the sweet relief of a slaughtered blister.

I lace my shoes back up and Ian hands me my bag full of fresh calories and water.

"Just eighteen miles to go!" he says. The sun still burns high in the sky and that mileage is the most manageable number I've heard since I started running three days ago. I feel a surge of excitement rush through me.

"We'll see you at Charlton Lake!"

He knows I've been looking forward to Charlton since the first step of the run, since I mapped out this plan months ago. It's been the light at the end of the tunnel through the first huge days—and the carrot I've chased that's kept me on schedule. To fall even a few miles behind would've jeopardized my plan.

And now it's the next place I'll see Ian. It feels almost close enough to touch.

Justin and I take off toward Rosary Lakes and it's like springs have been implanted into my legs. It's a gradual climb to the chain of lakes and I cruise up it.

I look up at the soaring pines that line the trail and down at the rich chocolaty soil beneath my feet. This part of the PCT overlaps with the Waldo 100k course, a race that I've been at every year since moving to Oregon. It's our local ultra, and someone from the Hunt reliably runs it every year. I've always paced, crewed, or raced it myself. Soon we'll run by the tree where a few years ago Eric stashed Skittles and a Coke so I could surprise our friend Tom while I was pacing him through the hottest miles of the race.

I remember running Waldo in August 2018, to cap off a summer of huge mountain adventures: the ninety-three-mile Wonderland Trail around Mount Rainier, multiday backpacks through the Trinity Alps, a fifty-mile run around the Three Sisters. I'd snapped a bone in my wrist when my foot caught a rock in the trail and sent me careening into a downed log during a loop around Three Fingered Jack on July 4—and with my doctor's blessing I spent the summer running in an unremovable brace, asking friends to tie my shoes and fasten my hydration pack while my brace got smellier by the mile.

It came off the week before Waldo, and the race was my first real run without it. While my arm had atrophied, my legs were hardened by the mountains.

"You're so strong from all of your summer adventures," my friend Lewis told me the week of the race. "Go celebrate that on Saturday."

I loved that way of thinking about a race, especially after breaking part of me. As a celebration of strength.

When I took off in the dim light of dawn, in a sea of headlamps, on the day of the Waldo 100k, I started to celebrate and play. My legs danced with the trail. My body flowed with the mountains. Each step I took was charged with gratitude and joy.

All day, I saw friends along the course. The same friends I'll see today. I shared miles with Eric from the Twins to Charlton Lake. High-fived Christian at the start. Cheered Evan into the finish. Got water and food from Joe and Callie at an aid station. Nothing could have wiped the smile off my face that day.

Having fun didn't mean I needed to take it easy or go slow. I still pushed myself to have my best day, but I held onto joy and let it propel me up and over the four mountains along the course—until I was charging toward the finish line on this very stretch of trail. I felt strong from the first to the last step, and I don't think it was unrelated to treating the event as a celebration of fitness, instead of a race to the bottom of the pain cave.

It's easy to remember the times in my life when running was a punishment and not a celebration. When miles have been a means of control. When I've turned to exercise as penance for my body.

There were times when I didn't train with any joy at all. When I let a fixation with data and results trump any fun I might have. When I chose workouts over friends. Running that way usually landed me on the sidelines with an injury. I remember when a physical therapist diagnosed me with an "injury party in my right leg" because I'd run through so much pain. It felt like anything but a party when I hung up my running shoes for months.

To run as a celebration of strength, and to run with joy, is a radically different way to run, and I feel how it has transformed me as an athlete and helped me get here, where I'm almost halfway across the state of Oregon.

Today feels like another celebration of strength. After another kind of breaking of me, the emotional shattering in the wake of losing my mom.

I think about all the miles that I put in to get ready for this run. All of the grief I've carried with me along the way. I started training for it in January, but I'd been training for it for years, really. Since I ran my first 50k in that urban park outside of Philadelphia seven years ago—and kept going.

I'm still bounding down the trail with Justin, and it's hard to believe the legs propelling me are the same legs that shuffled through the outskirts of Crater Lake in the dead of night. I haven't had anything resembling adequate rest and recovery since then, but I feel like an entirely different runner today. A stronger runner—which defies logic, since all I've done is battered my limbs with even more miles. I've been rebuilding myself through the rubble of this run.

On that second day, it was hard to believe I could make it to the next trailhead. But today, I really can see myself running across Oregon.

I look at my watch every few steps as we run toward Maiden Peak, knowing the halfway point is near. We're in one of my favorite parts of the forest. This wilderness is what I picture whenever I'm asked to envision my happy place. The fir trees are as high as twenty-seven of me, and bright green lichen cascades down the bark. This forest is a deep breath, a grounding, a stream of joy.

When the digits on my watch tell me I've hit 230 miles since Saturday, I stop and jump in the middle of the trail.

"Halfway!" I shout to every tree around me.

"Halfway," I repeat to myself. I press my hand into the closest tree, feeling the rough texture of the bark against my palm. Elation bursts through me as I think about how far I've come to get here.

I am here because I wanted to do something harder than anything else I've ever done—but I know that doesn't mean I need to suffer every step of the way.

February 2019
Willamette Pass, Oregon

I started hanging out with Ian just a few months after my mom's diagnosis. I was going through most of my days in a haze. Wading through the fog of cancer. I was probably trying to distract myself from the pain when I texted him to see if he wanted to ski.

Ian showed up in a tutu. It was my twenty-second ski day of the season and he decided that we should celebrate my "two-two" date of skiing with the appropriate attire. We hiked up the mountain while snow fell around us, Ian in poofy blue tulle and me in a sparkly red number.

He climbed in front of me and I giggled as I watched his tutu bounce with his steps through the stormy morning. He was ridiculous in such a charming way. He drops puns as naturally as he breathes, he shakes his hips at the faintest beat, and he has a flair collection that rivals the most colorful thrift store. I couldn't look away from his unabashed silliness.

The next time we hung out was with a group of seven friends. Ian crammed all of us into his aging Honda Pilot and we drove the seventy-five minutes up the pass to tour a local mountain on skis. He blasted Kesha and Sofi Tukker on the tinny stereo, and we shouted along to the music and threw our arms toward the pilled ceiling.

When we got to the trailhead, Ian dumped out a mesh sack full of flair for everyone to raid. He wore a silver sequin skirt that twirled with his hips. I had a bright metallic gold one on over my navy snow pants. I hopped into the skin track behind him, and he kept me cackling the entire hike up the ski hill, as he made jokes about our "human-powdered endeavor" and what a "flake" he was for forgetting gloves.

Each burst of laughter was a big exhale. I hadn't let myself laugh like that in weeks—I hadn't let myself have any fun. I hadn't felt like joy could live alongside my mother's cancer. But I thought of my mom back in Vermont, on her daily walks with friends. "It's what keeps me going."

Her daily dose of happiness was the permission I needed to go skiing in a gold skirt with a cute guy. Her walks with her friends were a prescription to chase joy myself.

As I climbed behind Ian, breathless from hiking and laughing, it was easy to feel why she needed those walks with her friends.

"I think Ian's your boyfriend fairy," Eli said, when we got back to our house at the end of the ski day. We were hanging all our wet gear on every stair rail and chair back. My side ached from laughing so hard. My shoulders relaxed from the clench that had gripped them for weeks.

"I haven't seen you like this since your mom got sick. And no matter what happens with Ian in the long run, he's exactly what you need right now."

Mile 236,
Willamette National Forest

We're on the north side of the Twins when we spot people running toward us—and hear them coming. I squint at the cheering pair of runners. It's my friends Sarah and Gracie, who have run in from Charlton Lake to meet us.

Sarah folds me into a jumping hug. Her blond hair flies all over.

"Emily!" she squeals. "Holy shit, look at you!"

Gracie is talking a mile a minute as she gives me a rundown of all the people waiting on the lake.

"Everyone is there!" she says.

"And you should know that Dilly just went on his first paddleboard ride," Sarah adds. I picture little Dilly, floating around the lake, looking at the water with his curious and mischievous gaze, with his one ear cocked to the sky, and grin at the thought.

We become a freight train of runners charging down the trail. More friends run out to meet us as we get closer. We're seven strong by the time I see a flash of sapphire water through the trees and know we've got just steps left for the day. We get to a fork in the trail and break with the PCT to head down to the shore.

The scene at the lake takes my breath away. Evan is hovered over a grill, with a tower of sausages, rolls, and condiments next to him. Huge coolers circle the campsite, and I don't need to open them to know they're packed full of good Oregon IPAs. A rainbow of tents sits on the shore of the lake. Joe has his PT table set up in case I need bodywork or a massage. There's a roaring fire with a dozen camp chairs circled around it. Nearly my entire running crew is here, along with many of their family members. Well over a dozen people total, including my friend Dan, who's been too injured to run with us for years now but was a huge part of my introduction to trail running in the Pacific Northwest.

"I heard about this and knew I couldn't miss it," he said. His sandy brown hair is still wet from swimming across the lake.

I remember meeting my Tuesday night running friends on my third week in Oregon. It was immediately clear that they were a special group of humans. We're a motley crew—who would never know each other without running. Middle-aged dads, sober vegans, conservative engineers, liberal high school teachers, and a thirty-five-year-old writer on a mission to run across the state of Oregon.

It's an unlikely group, but it works in the most beautiful way.

When I had to move out of my house a year after I moved to Eugene, I asked if anyone could help lug my stuff to my new apartment. The Hunt showed up en masse with pickup trucks and Honda Elements, and the entire move lasted all of seventeen minutes as they toted every box and piece of furniture into vehicles and drove three miles up the road.

My fourth day on the PCT feels like that seventeen-minute move all over again.

"What can I grill you?" Evan asks. He's a forty-seven-year-old dad and acts the part. We were on this same lake for his birthday run just a month and a half ago, when we ran thirty-two miles and then Evan grilled piles of food for us, despite the fact that it was his birthday. As soon as I told him I'd be stopping at Charlton for the night, he offered to do the same for me.

I'm bombarded by offers of food and beer as soon as I sit down. Sarah covers me in a sleeping bag, Andrew offers to fetch me a beer, and Evan brings me a piping hot kielbasa. I greedily eat it, washing down bites with a cold beer.

"Can I have another?" I sheepishly holler over to Evan—and he's by my side with a tong full of sausage before I can say "kielbasa."

Joe kneels next to me. He's been my physical therapist since I moved to Oregon, and when he heard about the run, he told me he'd be at Charlton with his table, ready to work on anything I might need.

"How's your body doing?" he asks.

"Honestly, it's pretty great," I say. "My right knee is a tiny bit aggravated, but nothing debilitating at all."

"Let's take a look at it," he says, and escorts me over to his table, which is surrounded by a mesh screen, just in case the mosquitoes are bad. They can be absolutely legendary in this wilderness, but tonight I don't notice any at all.

Joe kneads my muscles and makes small adjustments to my body as he goes.

"It's really amazing you're doing so well after over two hundred miles," he says. He shakes his head in disbelief as he kneads his thumbs into my calf. Joe is discerning with praise, and I know he's legitimately impressed that I've covered so many miles in four days.

When he's done, I walk back to the lounger and sit down surrounded by the buzz of my friends.

Time has been rendered meaningless out here and the days of the week are lost on me. My life immediately became the trail, and it seems like it's only in a parallel universe that people are still going to work and getting eight hours of sleep a night. But today, it feels like a Tuesday.

Callie comes over and crouches beside me. She brushes her long golden waves out of her face.

"Can I give you a massage?" she asks. "We can do it by the fire so you stay warm."

"I am definitely not going to refuse that offer," I tell her.

I let her walk me over to Joe's table, which she's moved so it's perched by the fire. The flames lick the black sky as I lie down. The camp chairs are full of my friends, and their laughter floats into the dark night. Callie starts working on my calves, her hands melting my stiff muscles into putty.

I am punch drunk with relaxation by the time she finishes. I get back in my chair and pull my sleeping bag up to my shoulders. The stars dance overhead. I imagine my mom following this run, texting Ian for hourly updates. It would make her so happy to know how my friends held me through the day.

My eyes are heavy with fatigue and I know I should go to sleep soon. But I don't move a muscle.

I glance into the dark forest behind me. I could still be running out there right now, my headlamp bobbing through the black night, just like it has done for the last three nights, and just like it will again tomorrow. I finished well before sunset, and it would've been easy to squeeze a few more miles into the day. I could have kept going until I was begging the trail to turn itself into an escalator.

But I know this night on the lake is going to carry me much farther.

Five

OUT OF THE WOODS

AUGUST 5, 2020
DAY FIVE—CHARLTON LAKE TO McKENZIE PASS
59 MILES, 6,870 FEET OF CLIMBING

Mile 248,
Three Sisters Wilderness

We are running through a maze of pine trees, and it feels like I'll never get out of the woods again. Forward my mail. Tell the DMV. I live here now.

The Charlton Lake party is over. It was back to business before the sun was up this morning. Andrew was outside the van in the blue light of dawn, ready to pace me through the first thirty miles of the day. The remnants of last night's lakeside barbeque feel like a frat house floor, sticky with beer and hazy memories.

I got to let loose and now it's time to lace back up. I have to run another sixty-mile day to get to my next stopping point at McKenzie Pass.

I hear Andrew padding down the trail behind me. His footsteps are steady in the soft dirt. I can picture him trotting along. His lanky frame, a beanpole in baggy shorts and loose shirt. His scraggly brown hair bouncing with his stride.

I've lost track of how many miles we've run in this forest, in this unending maze of firs. I look up and see my ten thousandth evergreen of the day. It's been nothing but trees and small pools of water tucked into the nooks of the forest.

"Have you been here before?" I asked Andrew, as we dipped into the woods at the start of the day, with cotton-candy clouds overhead.

"Never," he said.

It might be a new stretch of trail for both of us, but it quickly felt familiar. Evergreen after evergreen. Lake after lake. Fern after fern. Bend in the trail after bend in the trail, always revealing more of the same.

"You know what this makes me think of?" I ask Andrew.

I don't wait for him to respond before I am belting out Taylor Swift: "Are we out of the woods yet? Are we out of the woods yet? Are we out of the woods yet? Are we out of the woods?"

The song becomes the anthem of our miles. We wail it into the empty forest as the answer remains the same: no, we are not out of the woods yet.

Winter 2019
Eugene, Oregon

My mom started her clinical trial at Dana-Farber Cancer Institute in September. In October, she biked forty miles because she was feeling so good. In November, my aunt Mary told me I should come home. "I wouldn't wait," she said. In December, her oncologist delivered the worst news. The cancer had exploded. It had invaded new organs. The trial wasn't working. It was time to end her treatment.

The rapid deterioration of her health gave me whiplash.

My brain couldn't keep pace with it all. How had she gone from biking forty miles to careening toward her deathbed in a matter of weeks?

My mother was also shocked by her rapid decline. Her low spell had felt like another pothole in the road, not the end of her life.

When her oncologist gave her the news, she asked: "What about Doxil?" A type of chemotherapy that would act as a maintenance drug and help prolong her life.

Her voice was a whisper, whittled away by cancer.

"You can pursue Doxil, but it will offer less than a ten percent chance of helping," her oncologist told her.

My mom didn't ask the one question I couldn't stop thinking about. So, I called her oncologist. My heart was choking me. It was beating against my eardrums.

"I'm sure you gathered that my mom avoids the hardest questions," I said, my anxiety chopping each word into splinters.

"But I need to know. How much time do you think she has left?"

"It's hard to know these things for certain," her doctor said. "But I would be surprised if she makes it three months. It could be as little as a month from now."

I hung up the phone but her oncologist's words didn't go anywhere. I felt the familiar rush of hot tears. Another tidal wave crashing down on me. I'd lived here for the last year. Tossed around by the waves of cancer like a rag doll.

I needed a life preserver to save me, but the only thing floating by was "maybe a month left."

Mile 255,
Three Sisters Wilderness

I'm supposed to run past three of Oregon's most prominent volcanos later today, but right now, it feels impossible to believe that the mountains still exist.

I look for the hint of a tree line like a prayer on the horizon. But my prayer remains unanswered.

Andrew is still running behind me. His footsteps as dependable as the forested terrain.

"Pam's been asking about your run every day," Andrew says. "She sends very loud cheers from Eugene."

Pam is Andrew's mom and a quintessential mother. I met her carrot cake before I had the pleasure of meeting Pam herself, because she sends baked goods with Andrew for his biggest runs—and now for mine, too. A piece of her signature cake is wedged in my pack for a special treat.

The thought of Pam checking in with motherly excitement fills me with warmth. And then a swift rush of sadness hits when I think about how my own mom isn't here to do the same.

My mom was legendary with her check-ins during my big runs. They were fueled by equal parts motherly pride and motherly concern.

I remember calling her after my first big adventure run—a double-crossing of the Grand Canyon, which clocked in at just under fifty miles with over 10,000 feet of gain, including a massive 5,000-foot climb to get ourselves out of the canyon at the end of the long, hot day. As we climbed, we passed dozens of trailside stragglers, people who couldn't go another step because they were so walloped by the desert heat. We saw park rangers spending the evening hours tending to debilitating cases of dehydration and heat exhaustion—running Gatorade and space blankets down to the people splayed over boulders along the trail. It was sobering to witness the harsh reality of misadventure and imagine dealing with it even deeper into remote terrain.

"Do you realize how much could've gone wrong?" I asked my mom over the phone the next morning. I started rattling off a list of desert hazards. "Snakes! Sprained ankles! Heat! Dehydration! And if something had gone really wrong in there, the only way out would've been a helicopter ride!"

"I try not to think about it, Emily," she snapped back. She was supportive of me pursuing the things that made me happy, but I think sometimes she would have preferred if knitting or crossword puzzles were the activities that filled me with joy.

She didn't sleep much during my 100-mile efforts. She'd stay awake all night, refreshing my tracker and checking for updates from my crew, despite the fact that she knew she shouldn't expect news more than every seven or eight hours given the distance between aid stations and the spotty service in the mountains.

Her friends told me she would text and call them with constant updates during my longest runs. If they coincided with a school day, she'd keep popping out of her classroom to refresh my tracker and check for messages, poking her head into the classroom across the hall to give a thumbs-up that everything was okay.

"She was so proud of you—but that didn't stop her from worrying," they told me.

When she wasn't checking for updates, she was posting her own, usually on Facebook, at least seven to ten times per run. One of my favorite messages that she put up was before my first attempt of the Cascade Crest 100:

*"If someone thinking about you translates to speed, then Emily will be *flying* through every mile because I will be *obsessed* with her forward movement."*

I know she would be proud of me for tackling this run across Oregon—but also so worried about everything that could go wrong. Her sleep deprivation would've rivaled my own.

I imagine how many Facebook posts she'd share over the course of this multiday effort—she'd probably hit triple digits before I reached Washington.

December 2019
Eugene, Oregon

I packed up my car on Christmas Eve to drive to Vermont. I'd felt powerless since I hung up the phone with my mom's oncologist. Since my mom was diagnosed, really.

I couldn't do anything to stop the dominoes that kept falling and shoving my mom from diagnosis to deathbed. But I could drive across the country to see her.

I could get in my car and wrap my hands around the black leather of the steering wheel. I could cover 3,000 miles from Oregon to Vermont. I could press my foot on the gas pedal and carry my body over a dozen state lines, even if I couldn't do anything to save hers.

I didn't know how long I would be gone. I just knew that the only thing that made sense was to go.

I carried loads of my heaviest winter gear past the scrappy Charlie Brown tree that was tucked into the corner of our living room. It was my concession to Ian, who loves everything about Christmas, to do something to mark a holiday season that felt drained of every ounce of merriment. We thought we would wake up to it on Christmas morning, but instead, we'd start our holiday with cold asphalt and faded mile markers. Ian didn't hesitate before offering to join me for the cross-country trek.

I looked at the tree's scraggly branches, drooping beneath a string of blue lights. It was my one request for our sad Christmas display. Blue lights, just like my mom had always done.

I thought about her back in Vermont in a house that was stripped of all holiday cheer. She didn't want a tree this year, or any of her other holiday traditions. It was the first time I'd seen my mother greet Christmas with anything but bins of decorations, hours of carols and cookies, and weeks of joy. Her friends offered to bring her a small tree, so she could have something festive in the house, but she wanted nothing to do with Christmas. The empty holiday season felt like it had already shifted into mourning mode.

I Tetris-ed our gear into the back of my gray Toyota RAV4. I built a nest for Brutus on the back seat, piling blankets and sleeping bags for him to curl into.

Flying to Vermont wasn't an option with Brutus—and leaving him behind was even less of an option. He was too old and needed more care than I would leave to someone else for more than a few days. It was a decision that wasn't really a decision. And regardless of his age or needs, I couldn't imagine making such a hard trip without him. He may not have had the official designation, but there was no question that he was my emotional support dog. He'd been by my side or burrowed into my armpit for most every tear of the last year.

I surveyed the packed car, with down jackets piled on top of thick boots. As I looked at my duffel bag, I couldn't stop a wrenching thought: *Should I pack a black dress?*

I walked back inside and looked at my closet. I thumbed through the dresses hanging in the back. As I touched the fabric of a black one and imagined putting it on in Vermont, I felt the floor give out beneath me.

I understood that my mother was going to die soon. But packing clothes to wear to her funeral would make it feel more real than I could bear. I walked away from the closet in a daze, leaving the black dress swinging on its hanger.

Mile 270,
Three Sisters Wilderness

It's been nearly thirty miles and we are still in the woods. We're in the Groundhog Day of the PCT, repeating the same mile over and over again.

"I'm sorry you got such a dull part of the trail," I apologize to Andrew.

"Oh, it was great, it's all new," he said. Andrew can put a positive spin on most anything—and he's doing it again beneath our one-millionth fir tree of the day.

I look ahead, my gaze fixed on the gaps in the trees, searching for thinning forest and widening sky. I fantasize about breaking free of this dense forest and spilling out into an open meadow. But the only things I see are trees in every direction, growing up, down, and all around me.

December 2019
Oregon

Fat raindrops hit the windshield as we pulled out of Eugene. I locked my eyes on the asphalt and started to drive east. My tires plowed through a puddle and unleashed a spray of water.

I looked in the rearview mirror. I could almost see my mother's death, strapped into the back seat, settled in for every mile of the drive to Vermont. Its cold fingers digging into my shoulders. Its icy breath on my neck. The threat of it had never felt more real than it had since "maybe one month left."

As I watched the rain turn to snow on the windshield with our climb up the mountain pass, I expected my grief to snowball from Oregon to Vermont. Growing bigger and bigger with each state line we crossed. My body would tumble along with it, growing more and more consumed by grief as we got closer to Vermont and the reality of my mother's death.

Mile 272,
Three Sisters Wilderness

I squint my eyes. It looks like the sky is expanding through the trees. The slivers of blue are transforming into an open canvas.

"Is that . . . ?" I don't dare finish the sentence. I don't want to jinx anything. I look around. There's been no shortage of wood to knock on this morning.

"I think it's happening," Andrew whispers, like we're conspiring against the forest and we don't want it to catch us before we escape.

We run up a small pitch that carries us up a hill. The trees thin as we climb. The terrain opens up. The sky grows overhead. A meadow comes into view.

"Finally!" I cry to Andrew.

Breaking free of this forest feels nearly as exciting as yesterday's halfway point. In just a few steps, the trees shrink and the ground expands. My spirits lift with our first steps up into the alpine.

December 2019

We stayed at my friend Sarah's house just a few hours from Eugene that first night of our road trip across America. In the morning, Ian, Brutus, and I woke up before dawn and drove to the mountains to shake out our legs before a long day of highways. We pulled our skis out of the back and started climbing uphill in the dark. As we neared the top of the butte, sorbet clouds drifted across the sky. The climb opened up to a view of the Three Sisters, the dramatic trio of peaks buried in snow and framed by the pink sunrise.

We transitioned our skis into downhill mode and I let gravity carry me down the mountain. I floated across the fresh snow, feeling lighter as I carved my skis into the hill in big, playful swoops. Each turn of the descent was an unwinding.

We got back in the car and kept driving east. The snowy mountains gave way to high desert. James Taylor came on as we steered through fields of sage and cattle. His warm baritone transported me back to a concert that I went to with my mom. I saw her bobbing and singing along as James serenaded us. Her schoolgirl crush floated through her highest off-key notes. My heart lurched as "Fire and Rain" filled the car.

We drove ten hours to Salt Lake City and my brain went numb with the highway. Endless pavement stretched into the horizon. I stopped feeling anything. White noise hummed over the bellowing grief.

We slept on the floor of Ian's friend's house. In the morning, we climbed up Little Cottonwood Canyon, surrounded by a fishbowl of alpine ridges, mountains stretched in every direction, smothered in snow. We squiggled through the powder. Bouncing with each swoop of our skis. My heart rate raced with adrenaline instead of panic.

Back in the car, we rolled past streets stacked with Christmas decorations on our way to the highway. I thought of my mom in her empty house. The first Christmas morning of her life without anything to celebrate the holiday. The last Christmas morning of her life. A boulder sank into my gut at the thought.

After Utah, we thought we were done with our ski breaks until the Northeast. But while Ian was manning the steering wheel in Nebraska, I got on Google.

"Did you know we'll drive right past a ski hill in Iowa?"

It was closed for the day because of heavy rain. We bought umbrellas at Target and clicked into our skis on the man-made snow at the base of the 300-foot hill.

I skied through the slush with my zebra-print umbrella. My purple rain jacket zipped up to my chin. My damp hair flew behind me. I laughed as my skis sprayed me with water. I skated across the bumpy parking lot, back to the car and another long day of highways, where I'd reckon with what it would mean to cross the final state line into Vermont.

I savored how light I felt as my skis glided across the wet snow, gifting me with a sense of ease, if only for a moment in time.

Mile 273,
Three Sisters Wilderness

A rush of movement careens toward us.

It's Dilly and Firnie, my friend Alli's puppy, who happens to be almost identical in age, and, unbelievably, energy level to Dilly. They are pinballing between trees and wrestling in the middle of the trail in a tornado of feral puppy play. Their jaws latch onto each other's fur, flashing sharp puppy teeth.

Sarah, Alli, and Ian are cheering up ahead. I see gear and food laid out on a blanket covering the dusty ground. They hiked everything in from the trailhead a mile below. I take a seat in a camp chair and let Ian strip off my shoes and swap out my socks.

"Dilly met his play soulmate," he says.

"I see that!" I say, as I watch Dilly and Firnie tumble around in the dirt in a fit of tangled somersaults. Their puppy growls fill the air, like angry Ewoks in a feisty wrestling match.

"We had to physically separate them so they would nap for a few minutes," says Sarah. She tries to nuzzle Dilly's floppy ears as he bolts past.

The heat of the day beats down on me as I survey the scene for appetizing food. I grab cubes of watermelon and a triangle of a quesadilla. I take tepid bites. It's still a challenge to eat as much as I need.

"Andrew got exactly half a mile out of the woods all day," I report, with an apologetic laugh.

"It was great," Andrew protests. "It was almost all new trail to me."

Alli is standing next to her other dog, Riggins, a black and white border collie who is much more mature than the two scallywags tumbling around in a cloud of dust. Her brown hair is pulled into tiny pigtails that poke out beneath her hat. She's ready to share the next thirty-mile leg with me.

We take off and start running north together, with Riggs trotting along between us.

South Sister, the first of the three mountains in the trio of volcanos known as the Three Sisters, looms large before us. Lingering snow and glaciers sprawl from the 10,358-foot summit. The rugged slopes that were forged by fiery lava flows are a patchwork of slate, crimson, and charcoal rocks. The volcano melts into a golden field, baked by the summer sun.

South Sister is one of the most recognizable peaks in Oregon. I've probably seen this mountain hundreds or thousands of times in my life, but it has never looked so beautiful.

December 2019

As we got closer to Vermont, I thought about my mom traveling to see me when I lived in DC and then in Oregon. She made every visit seem like it was the highlight of her year.

Much like her obsessive posting during my races, she used Facebook to share detailed updates about her journeys from Vermont to get to me. She'd post a photo per layover, accompanied by a countdown tracking the minutes until she landed.

On the last trip out to Oregon, she snapped a photo in the Salt Lake City airport. A book cracked open on her lap. Her legs folded, with a Starbucks coffee cup tucked beside her.

"Can barely read, too excited," she said. "Only 4 hours and 17 minutes until I see my baby girl."

Mile 278,
Three Sisters Wilderness

So much has changed in just a few miles.

Bright purple lupine grows everywhere like a sea of wildflowers. Its sweet, earthy scent wafts through the air. The trail weaves through the meadow, and we run surrounded by lilac blossoms. We hop across a tumbling creek as Riggs laps cold water from the stream. We stay in the wide-open alpine, above the tree line, with a colossal mountain almost always in our line of sight. As soon as we circle South Sister, its sibling Middle Sister comes into view. Its summit is sharper and more abrupt than its southern neighbor.

I haven't seen Alli in weeks and she is full of adventure stories to share. And ideas to float out for future runs.

"I would love to do Soft Rock next summer," she says, referring to a 100-mile loop through the San Juan Mountains, a vast and rugged mountain range in Colorado.

"Oh, I want to run Soft Rock, too!" I cry. I picture us galloping through fields of columbine and paintbrush and plunging into icy blue alpine lakes.

I surprise myself with my excitement.

Right now, the cumulative toll of this trek is acute in my body. My legs are heavy with miles and I can't wait to stop running for the day and collapse in a camp chair—sitting sounds a million times better than taking my next step. It would be easy to swear off the sport forever, after running 270 miles in less than five days.

It's a reassuring sensation, to believe I'll want to run long distances again. To trust that any negative feelings won't be as lasting as they might seem during one moment in time.

December 2019

I wait until I'm on the other side of the Mississippi before I tell my mom I'm on my way to Vermont.

I knew she'd try to talk me out of it if I was still in Oregon. She never stopped trying to save me from the pain of cancer. It didn't matter that she was a sheet of paper on railroad tracks, attempting to block a steam engine from barreling ahead.

"You shouldn't," she says, when I let her know that I'm coming.

I know she's saying that to protect me. To throw her motherly shield around me. I know she's deeply depressed and mourning her life. But all I hear is my mother telling me, "don't come." When the only thing in the world that makes sense to me is to go to my mom.

When there's nowhere I need to be but with her. I am a child crying for my mother, and her words leave me wailing, desperate for the comfort of her arms.

Mile 282,
Three Sisters Wilderness

I hop over a small rock and the landing is a blow to my limbs. I dread the weight of the next step.

My legs feel like they've been shoved through a meat grinder. My muscles have been crushed and crumbled and chewed to bits.

I never want to run again. Forget Soft Rock and the San Juans. Forget every step after the bridge. I'm retiring from this silly sport as soon as I get to Cascade Locks. I can't believe I do this for "fun." Nothing feels fun about running on quadriceps that have been pulverized into hamburger meat. Nothing feels fun about blisters growing on every inch of my feet like a flesh bubble bonsai garden. Nothing feels fun about my brain turning into a mushy pile of porridge.

Fun would be sitting in a bubble bath with a hot cheese pizza and a seven-layer chocolate cake perched on the edge of the tub. Fun would be reading on the beach, in a gloriously reclined position, with a cold drink in hand. Fun would be watching a marathon of *The Bachelor* with my girlfriends, curled into a couch with chips and guacamole.

Running 460 miles in a week is not fun.

January 2020
Lincoln, Vermont

The Vermont sky was cold, gray, and indifferent when we rolled into the state. The trip felt like a cataclysmic rupture in my life. But the sky didn't flinch as I crawled up my parents' driveway. Small snowbanks from my father's plow lined the winding climb up to the house.

I parked and saw my father chopping firewood outside. He paused at the sound of a car pulling up, his axe hung on the upswing—before it fell into a piece of wood with a swift chop. He raised his hand in a slow wave; his face was stoic and as indifferent as the sky.

I walked up the rickety wooden steps I'd climbed millions of times before. It was a place that lived inside of me. But each step felt foreign. I could normally walk that ground blindfolded, but on that day, I didn't know how to navigate my next move.

The door creaked as I swung it open. One of the two golden cats hopped down from the hutch.

I slipped my shoes off and tiptoed down the hall in case my mom was sleeping. I turned the corner and saw her on the maroon couch, tucked beneath a blanket. Her eyes blinked open and met mine.

Her face didn't change when she saw me. The maternal excitement that had greeted me every single time I'd seen her for years was nowhere to be found.

I kept my eyes locked with hers, searching for something to hold onto. Her face remained hollow, my insides hollowed with it.

I'd already lost so much of my mom.

Mile 285,
Three Sisters Wilderness

This trail is a treasure hunt, and I've discovered ease in my stride again on this undulating stretch of dirt. My body and mind feel like they're rising and falling with the contours of the earth. My physical and emotional experience ebbs and flows through the highs and lows of each day, each mile, sometimes each step. Right now, my legs are flowing with the terrain. My heart swells at the sight of Alli and Riggins running in front of me, selflessly carrying me through this day. I look up at the horizon, where mountains spill into the distance. The sweeping view lifts me through the next step.

I cling to every moment that doesn't feel like a battle.

I think about how I've found, time and time again, that it's helpful to appreciate any unexpectedly good and easy moments during a long run—without getting too attached to the high of them. Like when drenching rain is in the forecast but I start under a quiet sky. Every dry step feels like a gift, especially when I know the next one could be through a torrent of rain. Or when I expect to get walloped by fatigue near the end of a race and I run with ease instead. I know to feel grateful for any mile that's not as hard as I think it will be.

I know to let the ease help me move forward, but to hold onto the highs lightly, because they can vanish as quickly as they appear.

January 2020
Vergennes, Vermont

Time had lost most meaning for me, but it was holiday break for the rest of the world and my friend Liam was visiting Vermont from San Francisco. Ian and I were staying with my aunt Mary while back in Vermont, because she had a finished basement apartment for us to sleep in with Brutus. Her house is close to Liam's family home, so we met him at a dive bar in Vergennes. We marched down into the basement space. The floor was sticky with yellow beer. The stale scent of it hung in the room.

It was karaoke night. Liam immediately signed up for a slot and performed a punk anthem that involved more shouting than singing. And then Ian said he had a surprise for us.

He walked up to the microphone and started singing Katy Perry in the deepest baritone he could muster.

He pulled his shirt collar down to reveal his thick chest hair and winked at us.

I laughed until my sides ached. I laughed until I couldn't breathe. I laughed until I was catching my breath.

Mile 290,
Three Sisters Wilderness

Alli reminds me to eat, and I pop watermelon gummies into my mouth. I wait for the quick rush of sugar that can be like jet fuel during a run.

I've had trouble eating since the first day in Southern Oregon. Food hasn't been as appetizing as I need it to be, which is a problem because when you don't eat enough, you're at risk of "bonking," as it's known in the running world, when your energy reserves get so depleted that your body can feel like it's incapable of physical movement.

I used to think of a bonk as a run-ending phenomenon. Once bonked, you stayed bonked, and there was no coming back from it.

So, when it happened before the halfway point of my first 100-miler, I was worried that I'd ended my race by not fueling with enough calories. I dejectedly crawled into an aid station on a dusty forest road and fell into a camp chair that my crew had toted in. I let my body fold in on itself, collapsing my head into my hands.

"I'm dragging," I told my friend Jason. I ran my finger over my forearm, feeling the crystals of salt caked on my skin.

My friend Meredith crouched at my side and asked what sounded good for food. I could only respond with a defeated stare.

"Let's get you something hot and salty," Jason said.

They brought me slices of cheese quesadilla with mounds of guacamole on top. For over fifteen minutes I sat there, letting my heart rate come down until I was ready to eat again. It was longer than I'd ever stayed at an aid station before, since every minute is on the clock. Not just when you're actually running, but every time you stop to eat, refill your hydration pack, or change your socks and shoes.

As I lingered, food became more appetizing and I hungrily ate the quesadilla, filling my body with salt, fat, and calories. I felt my energy shifting. I'd been a sputtering car, limping along on fumes. And now, my tank was full again.

"I think I'm ready to try and get back out there," I said.

I walked over to the forest road, which continued to pitch uphill into the hot September day. I started climbing and it felt like I had a new pair of legs beneath me. I'd thought my run was over. But I was back on the course, marveling at how a low that had felt so hopeless could pass, and I could keep hiking up the next hill.

January 2020
Burlington, Vermont

My mom had a meeting with her oncologist to discuss her next steps toward palliative care.

I drove to the hospital to meet my parents. I sat in the waiting room before they got there, a notebook tucked beneath my hands. My fingers drummed against the soft cover. I looked up at the clock, as if it could answer anything.

I heard the door open. My father rolled my mother into the waiting room in a hospital-issued wheelchair. Her face was pale, her eyes distant.

I stood up and walked over to her side. I touched the arm of the wheelchair and bent down until our eyes were level.

"Hi, Mom," I said. Her eyes met mine with a glassy stare.

She started to say something to me but her voice was muddled. It sounded like she was speaking underwater.

"I'm sorry, Mom, can you say that again?" I said. My pulse ticked up. I white-knuckled my notebook.

My dad interrupted: "She just started talking like this today."

A nurse jogged over. The meeting never started. My mother was rushed to the emergency room several floors down.

My head raced as fast as my heart. Machines beeped and I wondered what they were saying, if they were announcing a countdown to the end. My mom stared at the ceiling in silence, and I thought about how I would do anything to erase all of it. To go back to the winding dirt roads of Lincoln and run beside her through fresh snow. I wanted to take us back to a time when cancer didn't pierce every breath. I wanted to be anywhere but here, where the only thing I could feel was my mother's death descending, shrouding everything in a hopeless darkness.

Mile 293,
Three Sisters Wilderness

I am running through the black obsidian glass that cascades from the flanks of Middle Sister when I remember advice that the current record holder, Brian Donnelly, gave me before the run.

I reached out to Brian when I was getting ready for my attempt and told him about my plans to run across Oregon and to go after the FKT.

"I'm in such awe of your run," I said. "If you have any words of trail wisdom, I'd love to hear them."

He responded with a kind and encouraging note back. He promised I was about to have one of the most challenging and rewarding runs of my life. And then he offered a nugget of trail wisdom.

"Time and distance are sanctuaries," he said. "Everything that goes wrong will have time to change."

I think about his words as I run through the glassy rock that rises and falls around the trail like a rolling sea.

I remember running through the unending woods this morning, passing tree after tree and lake after lake. It felt like I was stuck in that forest, my running and life forever entangled with the roots of trees that were buried beneath the trail. I think about how one mile can feel impossible, and the next can feel like a gift.

I think about the fear and grief I've lived through for the last year and a half, through my mother's sickness and death. And the pain that I'm still living through now. How my fate has often felt sealed in the black hole of grief. How I've found joy and calm through the storm of cancer and loss. How grief ebbs and flows like the undulations of this trail. How change has been as constant as the dirt beneath my feet.

January 2020
Burlington, Vermont

My mother had a stroke. A common, and horrific, side effect of treatments that have a higher risk of blood clots.

She was moved from the emergency room to the neurology floor after an excruciating all-nighter. "We've got to get her onto oncology," my brother said. And I hated that he knew which floor was better.

Her body was scanned. Her body was held in the hospital. Her body was being taken over, more and more, by cancer. Her bowels were blocked, and her doctor said she would stay in the hospital until that changed. I lost track of what her most pressing health issue even was. The stroke. The cancer. The bowels. It was an endless and rapid deterioration of my mother.

My aunts Julie and Martha came to visit. They walked in and peeled off their thick winter jackets and gloves. My mom was sleeping, tucked beneath a thin hospital blanket, her cheek resting on the pillow. Julie gave me a tight hug and then Martha wrapped her arm around my shoulder and pulled me in. We rocked together, in silence, and then Martha started to talk.

"Do you remember when your mom ran around town in a helmet?" She giggled.

I laughed. My mom had been training for a triathlon at the time and wanted to do what's called a "brick" workout, where you stack two of the three triathlon sports together to condition your body to endure the demands of multiple sports in one race.

My mom had started her workout with a bike ride and then transitioned to a four-mile run around town—but she forgot to take off her helmet for the run and unknowingly jogged the four miles through the streets of Bristol with a helmet strapped on her head. When she finished the run and realized her gear blunder, she snapped a selfie and posted it on Facebook to poke fun at herself—and her very safe run around town.

I was breathless with laughter by the time we'd rehashed the whole thing. My belly ached as I pictured my mom, beaming away in her running clothes and a helmet.

"That smile of hers," my aunt Martha sighed.

I looked over at my mom, quietly asleep, the blanket rising and falling with her slow breath. Her face hung limp, pressed against the hospital pillow.

I thought about her smile and molten grief seethed inside me.

The idea that her smile would soon disappear was enough to pull me under. I was a rag doll again, flailing as "maybe one month" left me to drown. We were already two weeks into that month.

Frantic sobs rolled through my body, building from the deepest part of my core and spilling out. Just two minutes ago, I'd been laughing so hard I couldn't breathe.

The waves of cancer and grief kept tossing me around, from frothing despair, to weightless ease, to flailing beneath the surface, gasping for air, grasping for anything to hold onto, to floating in a calm sea, catching my breath, waiting for the next wave to hit.

Mile 297,
Three Sisters Wilderness

A sharp ache shoots up my lower leg as my foot hits the ground.

I wince and brace myself for the next step.

A cold gust of wind charges past us, and I whip my head around to look back at North Sister, the last of the three volcanos that I'll travel past today. The most violent mountain of the trio. Its summit is straight from Mordor, wild cliffsides and towering spires in every direction. The mountain is a spear on the horizon.

I remember starting this morning under a pink sky, before plunging into the woods for hours.

I look back again.

The sky is darkening over the sharp edges of the mountain. Black clouds swarm the summit. Thunder grumbles over North Sister. The forecast had shown nothing but blue skies and warm temperatures before I started. But things can shift quickly in the mountains.

And now, a storm is brewing.

Six

THROUGH THE STORM

AUGUST 6, 2020
DAY SIX—McKENZIE PASS TO BREITENBUSH LAKE
61.1 MILES, 8,878 FEET OF CLIMBING

Mile 305,
Mount Washington Wilderness

Everything around me feels like a threat.

When I woke up this morning and saw a swirl of pink sunrise floating across the sky, I wanted to believe the storm warning was a joke.

Eric told me on Tuesday that a storm could be coming when he handed me Dairy Queen on the flanks of Diamond Peak.

"Have you seen the weather for Thursday?" he'd asked, in a way that suggested I wouldn't like what I saw. When I started the run, there was nothing but sun and summer temperatures in the forecast.

"It looks . . . cold and wet," he went on.

My skin was gritty with salt when he told me this. I was wearing split shorts and an airy tank. And gulping icy Powerade like the greatest gift in this one precious life is a cold beverage. It seemed like a prank, that I could be freezing cold and soaking wet just two days later—without voluntarily jumping into a glacial lake for relief from the scorching heat.

Now, charcoal clouds swell overhead. A cold breeze rushes through pine needles, picking up speed like it's just getting started. The sky is darkening. The rain starts falling. The temperature starts dropping.

This was already set to be one of my longest and hardest days, with sixty-two miles and nearly 10,000 feet of climbing past three of Oregon's largest mountains—Mount Washington, Three Fingered Jack, and Mount Jefferson. But every mile feels like a descent into the belly of the day.

The ground is littered with sharp lava rock, as black as the sky. Mounds of obsidian glass rise and plummet around the trail like violent waves. I imagine falling and can almost feel the rocks gashing my flesh.

I take another step on the loose, rocky footing. It's like running over a pile of jagged softballs. The uneven terrain cranks my ankle and pain charges up my shin. I suck in a sharp inhale as my foot collides with the ground.

I don't know what's going to be harder to get through today—the mounting ache in my lower leg or the growing storm overhead.

January 2020
Burlington, Vermont

I'd been away from Oregon for three weeks and I was feeling it on a cellular level. Being in Vermont was hard for the obvious reasons. My mom was dying, and being back meant confronting that undeniable reality. This trip had been especially brutal, with the emergency hospitalization for a cancer-triggered stroke, her resistance to my presence, and her unremitting depression as she had to accept that hope wasn't going to save her. She'd approached cancer with astounding courage, joy, and determination—and after all that, she was still going to die.

Being in Vermont was even harder because Jess was also getting sicker. Her illness felt like it was on the same rapid downward spiral as my mom's, with unending bad scans, exploding cancer cells, and failed treatments. She even suffered a small stroke just days after my mom's. Our small family was getting ravaged by cancer. There was no escape from it. Nowhere to catch my breath. The longer I was in Vermont, the deeper cancer dragged me down.

In another life, my brother would have received my undivided support while Jess was sick. And in yet another life, we would have weathered the storm of our mother's cancer together, leaning on each other to stay upright.

But that wasn't the life we were living. The reality was that dueling bouts of cancer were attacking our family from every angle and there was no refuge for any of us. I couldn't leave the hospital and collapse at Jameson's because he was already on the ground. He didn't need my pain layered on top of his own. Our mother had always been the first line of support for both of us. We didn't have that kind of relationship with our father. So, as she slipped further away from us, we both felt stranded.

When my mom got sicker in November, a family member suggested that I move back to help with her care. But the idea made me squirm with anxiety.

I couldn't imagine spending every day watching my mother die without my own support system to keep me afloat. I thought about people who drop everything to fill that role. I hated that I couldn't be that person. If I tried, I would drown.

I felt like the worst daughter in the world. I knew the challenges of caretaking were nothing compared to what my mom was facing. I knew she would give up everything for me. But I never offered to move back, and she never asked me to.

That three-week trip was the longest visit I'd made back to Vermont since my mom's diagnosis, and it felt like it. My battery light was blinking red, my energy was dangerously low, and I had nothing to plug into to recharge.

Her medical team said she probably had several weeks left, maybe even a few months, so I started to think about leaving. I felt assured that there would be plenty of time to come back. I believed I would be there when it really mattered.

When I saw whiteout blizzards in the forecast, I decided it was time. We'd narrowly avoided closed highways on our way east, and I didn't want to get stuck in Nebraska or the Dakotas for days. I needed to get home, not wind up sitting out a storm in a roadside motel. So, we packed up our things and were ready to go. My mom's doctor said she'd recovered from her stroke and was stable enough to be discharged later that day.

I sat next to my mom's bed and told her my plan. Her gaze had softened since I first arrived, a surrender to the reality she was facing.

I could see how fatigued she was. This wasn't how she wanted to live. "I've spent time with my family," she'd told a hospice worker a few days earlier, slowly looking around the room at my brother, my father, and me. "That's everything I need." I'd listened to her utter those words with my inner lip clenched and quivering between my teeth, trying to contain the hurricane brewing inside me.

"Do you want me to wait until you leave the hospital?" I asked her.

She shook her head.

"You'll be back," she said. Her speech was still slow and slurred from the stroke. She had to search for each word.

"Of course," I said. I held her hand in mine.

I walked out of the room, my heart a rock in my stomach. I knew why I was leaving. But it didn't make me feel better about the fact that I was walking away from my mom while she was dying. I had no idea how quickly that rock would turn into regret.

There are so many memories that I've lost to time throughout my life. But the moments where I know I could've been a better daughter to my mom have stayed with me with searing clarity.

Mile 309,
Mount Washington Wilderness

The threats around me grow more visceral with the miles.

My shin pain was a whisper yesterday, but now it's screaming as I run through the lava field—decibels increasing with each step. I tell myself it's just the footing and once we're back on soft, smooth dirt, it will feel better. I try to push the pain out of my head. *It's only temporary,* I think. *It will get better soon.*

Time and distance are sanctuaries, I repeat my mantra from yesterday.

But each step shatters the myths I am telling myself. This pain isn't going anywhere. It's my shadow on this sunless day.

The weather is also devolving. It feels more like the middle of December than the sixth day of August. The temperature has dropped forty degrees since yesterday.

I look up at Mount Washington as we jog past the volcano. Tendrils of fog swirl around the summit, its rocky spires slipping in and out of sight as the storm swells over the peak. The mountain stabs the charcoal sky. It looks like a warning. The gargoyle flashing its teeth outside the castle. Telling me that the worst is yet to come.

January 2020
Boise, Idaho

I'm in the parking lot of a food co-op in Boise, Idaho, less than forty-eight hours after leaving the hospital, when I get the call.

It's my brother.

"Mom is getting moved to the hospice home."

His words hit me like a battering ram.

My mom didn't get discharged from the hospital that day. She went to Burlington for a doctor's appointment about setting up palliative care, and she never went home again. *She will never go home again*, I think. I picture the closets full of her clothes. The photo frames full of memories. The depression in the couch, where she read her last book. She'll never touch any of it again. I blink in shock.

I look around the parking lot. My eyes burn with sleeplessness. We drove from Vermont to Idaho in less than two days. On the first night, we didn't stop at all, taking turns driving and napping in the passenger seat. The next night, only for a few hours at a roadside motel in Wyoming. I was so desperate to get back home that my foot barely left the gas pedal. The same distance had taken us five full days in the other direction.

I look across the parking lot to the highway thick with traffic. We are still seven hours from Eugene.

I don't know what to do. My heart is choking me. My head pounds.

We could turn around now. But neither of us could pull the same shifts at the wheel. We wouldn't get back to Vermont for at least three or four days, even driving at our maximum limit. And the idea of driving back across the entire country when I can barely see straight makes me want to collapse in this parking lot and give up forever. We could finish the drive to Oregon—and I could almost immediately get on a plane and make the trip back to Vermont. Nothing feels like the right choice. Every decision feels like I already made the wrong one.

I've been beelining toward the finish line, where I could finally rest. And that finish line just went up in flames.

The floodgate rips open. My tears are an angry river, currents of grief and regret frothing in an indistinguishable mess of emotions.

I am crying because my mother is dying. I am crying because I left her.

Mile 318,
Santiam Pass

The storm is ratcheting up when we get to the intersection with Highway 26.

Semitrucks scream past, plowing through roadside puddles. Motors rattle as the trucks climb Santiam Pass. It's a jarring contrast to the quiet wilderness I've been submerged in for days. We wait for a break in traffic and then dash across the highway.

Nicole is waiting on the other side of the road with her van idling to take me to my first crew stop of the day, which is probably less than a quarter mile from the trailhead and easily walkable, but I don't turn down the chance to sit in a dry car for a few seconds. Her windshield wipers are fighting the pounding rain.

"The crew is over there." She points across the parking lot. "Get in!"

My body is quivering with chills and my flimsy jacket is soaked through. Her van is blissfully warm and I never want to leave the blowing heat ever again.

I strip off my wet gloves and rub my hands together, trying to bring life back to my numb fingers.

"You're amazing, you're my hero, you're doing so great." Nicole is talking as fast as her wipers are swiping.

We pull up to Ian's van and I see a tarp pitched over food and gear.

I duck inside the van and peel off my wet layers. Ian unties my sopping laces and hands me a fresh pair of shoes and socks. I fondle the dry shoes with longing. I wish I could hold onto this feeling for the next forty-five miles. My fingers are wrinkled and white from the rain.

I slip under a sleeping bag and Ian hands me ramen. I burrow into the warmth of the down and cradle the bowl of hot broth. I warn myself not to get too comfortable. The storm is picking up outside the van, and I need to force myself back into the thick of it soon.

I remember running the Cascade Crest 100 during its own August storm, when rain and wind battered the ridgelines along the course. Each aid station had a firepit set up, and runners would crowd around it like moths to a flame to get relief. Many runners decided to end their races in front of the fire. It took a Herculean effort to walk away from the heat each time. To leave what was comfortable and plunge back into the storm.

Eric asks me if I'm going to bring an actual rain jacket—a piece of gear I've never run in before, even in the thick of drenching Oregon winters. A piece of gear that felt ridiculous to pack when I was getting ready on a sunny July day.

"I think I might," I say.

I look out at the storm through the van door and draw in a deep inhale. I won't see Ian or this van for another thirty miles. Which will take me at least eight to ten hours to cover, with more mountainous terrain ahead. This is my last chance to swap out gear or grab any extra layers until well past nightfall.

I pull on my teal rain jacket and a fleece headband. I grab a dry pair of gloves from a bin beneath the bed. I step out of the van and start jumping up and down to keep my body heat up. I wrap my arms in a tight hug around my upper body and rub the glossy sleeves of my coat.

Is this enough? I wonder. *Is this too much?*

I hate thinking that I might make the wrong choice and have no way to change it.

I zip it up to my chin and head into the storm.

It only takes a mile for me to realize that the rain jacket is not enough—nor are any of my other layers.

My headband is soaked through. My fingers are numb in my wet gloves. I reach down and touch the fabric of my spandex shorts. I could wring a glass of water out of them.

A gust of wind plows into me, like I'm getting backhanded by the abominable snowman. I twist my face away from the cold slaps of air.

We're climbing through another burn zone toward Three Fingered Jack. Blackened tree trunks prod the dark sky. Ferns flail in the wind. The landscape storms around us.

The rain is falling from the sky in sheets. It's saturated every piece of my clothing, and now it feels like it's seeping through my skin, too. I can feel this storm drill all the way to my bones.

It's penetrated everything I brought to protect myself. I am stripped of every layer of defense. The storm rages on and I feel every blast of it.

January 2020

I board the plane to Vermont like I'm sleepwalking.

I find my seat and check the numbers on my ticket three times before I trust myself to sit down. We take off. The plane grumbles into the sky. I stare at the blue vinyl of the next row.

I hear a voice like it's underwater and look up. The flight attendant is standing over me. She makes eye contact. "What can I get you?" she asks. I register a pile of airline snacks on her cart.

I turn to the man next to me and say, "What did you get, babe?"

He stammers. "Um?" He looks at me like I'm a threat. Like he doesn't want to sit centimeters away from me. Like he wants the emergency exit out of this row.

I stare at him. It's not Ian sitting next to me. Ian couldn't be sitting next to me. Ian is still in Eugene. He'll be on his own flight tomorrow. But I couldn't wait because my mom is dying and I have to get back to her in time for her to know I'm there. The reason I'm on the plane is the unshakable nightmare on repeat in my head. Consuming so much of me that I can confuse a total stranger for the man I sleep next to every night.

Mile 324,
Mount Jefferson Wilderness

I can't see anything, but I feel more than I can bear.

Fog smothers everything around us. The mountains, the lakes, the shrubs, the stumps of fire-ravaged trees. The earth is shrouded in a thick layer of mist.

Rain assaults the ground. Small puddles pool on the trail as the water falls too fast for the dirt to absorb. The landscape is wide-open, with nothing to shelter us from the raging storm.

I pull my hood tighter around my face. Raindrops spill over the edge of the hood and run into my eyes. I fumble to wipe them away with my numb fingers. I fantasize about dry pajamas and think longingly of the blasting heat in Nicole's van. I try not to think about how many hours stand between me and relief. It's too many to offer me a single ounce of comfort.

But it's as hard to ignore the weather as it is my shin. Each step into the sopping earth sends mud and pain shooting up my leg.

"I'm sorry, I need to stop again," I say to Eric and Emily, my pacers through this section. Eric is with me all day and Emily is running thirty miles with us. I hoist my foot up onto a log and dig my fingers into my shin. I keep doing this, hoping the right touch will magically massage the pain away.

"Of course," Eric says, in a reassuring tone. But as I work on my shin, I see my friends blowing hot breath into their hands and bouncing up and down for warmth. I hate that they got stuck with such a hard day—and I hate that I'm making it worse by asking them to stand around while I deal with my shin.

We start running again. The massage did nothing. Every time my foot hits the ground, sharp pain rockets up my leg like lightning flashing.

The pain is as big as the sky. It's the punctuation to every step. I don't know how I can keep going.

January 2020
Burlington, Vermont

My dad picks me up from the Burlington airport. I know he hasn't had a sip of alcohol, but he drives like he's drunk. He blows through stop signs and blares his horn at cars merging into our lane.

An old person crosses the street in front of us.

"Get out of the way, you asshole!" he yells.

He starts to mutter. "You should be the one dying."

I flinch. I want him to stop. His anger is terrifying and unsettling.

But I also recognize the rage that's exploding out of him. I remember the day that Ian missed a turn on the way to the coast, and I shouted at him like I'd caught him with his dick in another woman.

I remember going for a run a few weeks ago and seeing an elderly woman, gray and wrinkled with age. The sight of her triggered a flash flood of loathing. I glared at her as hate boiled inside of me. Why did she deserve to get old and my mother didn't?

I got home and yelled "FUCK" into the empty corridors of the house. It echoed through the hallway. The sharp edge of the curse vibrated against the walls and taunted me—reminding me that there was no place for my rage to land.

I could be furious that my mom didn't get to grow old, that my mom was dying decades sooner than she should—but there was no justice to be found. No way to right the wrong. Nowhere for this hot pain inside of me to go.

Mile 336,
Mount Jefferson Wilderness

I'm scaling a bald ridgeline. The hillside plummets into a foggy abyss. The wind barrels into me and nearly blows me off the ledge. I press my fingers into the earth to steady myself.

Another gust slams into me. I crouch my body closer to the earth to stay upright.

"This is fun," I shout to Eric and Emily. "I've felt emotionally flattened by this storm for hours—but now it's actually trying to knock me down."

"What?" Eric screams back. He can't hear me through the wind.

The driving rain has been relentless for hours. The temperature feels like it's hovering just above freezing. The raindrops are ice on my flesh.

I think about checking my watch, but I know it won't help. It feels like we've been in this storm for days and still have days to go. Time feels hopeless.

I try to think of when I've felt this irreparably cold before and can't. I think about the biting cold of Vermont winters, when the temperature would fall seventeen degrees below zero and my nose would turn white with frostbite. I think about running through Oregon rainstorms and fantasizing about hot showers. I think about that August storm at Cascade Crest.

Cold is a familiar sensation. But I've never felt so inescapably stuck in it, so hopelessly far from relief. The storm is a labyrinth, and there's no shortcut out of it.

We turn a corner in the trail and run past a chalky gray lake, speckled with thousands of splashes of raindrops. A cluster of colorful tents sits on the lakeshore—probably thru-hikers who decided to seek refuge from the storm.

I think about knocking on one of the nylon doors and inviting myself inside for a cup of hot chocolate and a few minutes of cocooning into a sleeping bag.

All I want is a one-way ticket out of my misery.

But there's only one way through this day.

January 2020

My mom was coherent when she arrived at the hospice home. Her brother visited. Her teacher friends showed up with flowers. Jameson barely left her side.

"She's awake and alert," he texted. "She smiled at a joke this afternoon."

"She said to take a couple of days to rest in Oregon," he went on. "The nurses don't think there's any need to rush."

I called the nurses at the hospice home multiple times a day to check in on her while I was back in Eugene. To ask what signs they saw of her slipping from life to death. I was desperate to get back while she was still coherent. To make sure that the last time she saw me was anything but me leaving her. To make sure I had a chance to say everything I needed to say. I hadn't even started drafting a final goodbye.

The nurses were gracious and patient. No one can predict the trajectory of death, they told me. But they shared what they were noticing. And the signs of the end of life that hadn't shown up yet.

On a layover between Portland and Burlington, my brother texted me. "I want to be honest, Emmy. She's taken a turn. I don't know if she'll be awake when you get here."

I was aware of the passing of every second between that layover and the airport in Burlington. From the airport to the hospice home. When my father missed a turn. When the door was locked when we walked up to it. He banged on it with both fists, shouting for someone to let us in.

By this point it was late at night. I jogged down the hallway and slipped into her room in the dark. I crouched by her bedside. Her eyes were shut. Her breathing was steady. I touched her hand and whispered to her. My heart still racing as my body settled into stillness.

"I'm here, Mom."

Her eyes blinked open and met mine. I searched them for an answer. "See me," my gaze pleaded with hers.

Another second and they were shut. I'd never see them open again.

Mile 345,
Mount Jefferson Wilderness

Night descends over us. The darkness swallows us whole. A haunting silence settles over the forest.

The sun never came out. Not a single ray of light touched our skin. The sky faded from gray to black.

The rain eases but it's replaced by the damp cold of night. Every inch of fabric on my body is still wet and clings to my skin. Goose bumps prickle up my arms and legs. I think about how much energy I've burned today, as my body temperature battled the cold, rain, and wind.

I scour the woods for any sign of Ian. A headlamp or a hint of voices. But the forest is as endlessly dark as the day.

January 2020
Burlington, Vermont

I think about what I've heard about death. Lines in obituaries about a peaceful passing. About being surrounded by love and family. About how there was no suffering.

But my mother's death did not feel peaceful. It felt like the earth rupturing beneath me, my body slipping into the fault line.

When her breath disappeared, mine turned into a storm. I collapsed beside her bed and heaved. Every inhale was a desperate prayer, pleading for my mother to come back to me. Every exhale was a guttural howl, charged with anguish and fear. In one breath, my entire world collapsed.

The woman who had been my harbor was gone. Forever. I was unmoored and alone, in a heap on the linoleum floor.

My mother died surrounded by love and family. But I can assure you, there was suffering.

There is still suffering.

Mile 347,
Mount Jefferson Wilderness

I am battered when I finally see the faint glow of a headlamp through the trees.

I hear cheers from Ian and Gretchen as they spot our lights bobbing through the forest. I halfheartedly wave but can't choke out a response. We are a trio of wet, frozen rats hauling ourselves out of the depths of a swamp. Shoulders slumped. Feet dragging. Bodies and spirits beaten down by the miles and the storm. Voices ragged from shouting through the wind.

I stumble up to where Ian has laid out the gear he carried in from the trailhead. I peel off my damp layers. It's a battle to wrench my body out of the wet clothing. I pull on the fleece-lined pants that Ian brought me and melt into them.

I slide into the sleeping bag and lay my body flat against the ground, a bowl of ramen perched on my chest. Tendrils of steam unspool into the dark night.

I shut my eyes. *Just for a second*, I whisper to myself. I don't know how long it is until I hear someone's voice and jolt awake. More than the second I promised myself. I look up at the black sky and feel myself sink back to sleep.

I stay there, cocooned into my sleeping bag on the ground. Fading in and out of consciousness. Like nodding off in class. I'll hear someone's voice, jolt awake, and pretend it never happened, then fight the next descent. But it's a losing battle.

I know I can't actually fall asleep right now. As soon as I got in, we decided to trim a few miles off the day, but I still have another ten miles to go before the next spot where I can stop for the night. I have to cover another ten miles if I want any shot at the record.

I'm drifting toward the siren call of sleep again when I hear Eric through the haze.

"Emily, what do you think about leaving in the next few minutes?"

I blink my eyes open through the heavy tug of drowsiness. I see Eric, standing above me in his dry running gear, poles pressed into the ground. I want to throw my bowl at him. He just paced me nearly fifty miles through the worst weather my running shoes have ever met, and he's ready to keep going—and I am thinking about hitting him with a blunt object.

I draw in a long inhale. I sit up, my sleeping bag still pulled tight over my legs. My brain is groggy with drowsiness. I look down the trail, which winds out of sight into the dark woods. There's no part of me that wants to take another step on that trail.

I force myself out of the sleeping bag, pressing my hands into the cold earth to stand up. I grab my poles from Ian to steady my tired and pummeled body.

I stumble over to Eric.

"I guess I'm as ready as I'll ever be," I say.

He cheers and whacks his poles together.

"This is how records are won!" he yells.

I want to cry. But even a single tear feels like it would take more from me than I have left to give.

January 2020
Williston, Vermont

The morning after my mom died, I blinked my eyes open to a gray winter day. The landscape matched the despair I felt—bare trees stripped to their spindly trunks, snowy hillsides covered in skeletal shells of maples. The sky was cold to look at.

My mother is gone.

The fragments of my heart sank through me. It felt like they would stay there forever, my heart irreparably broken by the loss of my mother. I would live with the shards of glass inside me; the pain would pierce every breath I took.

I blinked again—aware of my inability to do more than that. I lay in bed, staring out the window at the bleak winter day, feeling the grayness that seeped inside and settled all the way into the marrow of my bones.

My mother is gone forever. I don't have a mother anymore. I will never see my mother again.

I could physically feel the hole inside me. When she left, she took part of me with her. I blinked again, in disbelief that anyone has ever found a way to keep going through such searing heartache.

Mile 351,
Mount Jefferson Wilderness

Eric and I step back onto the trail in the dead of night. The forest is a maze of shadows.

We are picking our way down from Woodpecker Ridge when we hear a low rumble, like thunder building over the mountains. I look up at the sky; it's finally quiet. The calm after the storm.

The rumble gets louder as we descend.

"The river," I gasp to Eric.

We make it down to the banks, where violent currents of water charge the drainage. It looks impassable. A fall would pull my body under, thrashing it against slick boulders as it tumbled downstream.

I prod my poles into the rushing water and plunge one foot in. The shock of water, flooded by snowmelt and icy rain, sends chills up my spine.

I look across the raging water to the trail on the other side, paralyzed by the idea of taking the next step.

January 2020
Williston, Vermont

I stumbled downstairs to my brother's kitchen. White walls met white carpet. The plush couches were covered in pillows. Gold shelves were lined with wedding photos. The house screamed Jess from every surface.

Jameson was on the other side of the kitchen island when I walked around the corner. His face crumpled when he saw me walk in. I crossed the room and wrapped him in a hug.

We stayed there, crying together.

"I don't want to do anything, but I keep thinking about what Mom would do," Jameson said.

He shifted his glasses to rub his eyes.

"I think we should do what Mom would do."

I thought about my mom, doing laps around the woodstove when she was recovering from her surgery. Walking snowy dirt roads with friends after every chemotherapy session. Biking along Lake Champlain after she found out the cancer was still there.

I nodded slowly. He didn't need to say anything else. We wordlessly got ready to go outside. We drove from Jameson's house to the closest ski hill. We got out of the car and slid into our skis. The biting winter air nipped at my nose. I tucked my face deeper into my down jacket.

We started walking uphill together. I felt the shards of my heart tearing into me with every step.

Mile 357,
Mount Jefferson Wilderness

I thought I'd reached the limit of what I could push through at least thirty-seven miles ago—but the PCT keeps throwing more at me. The storm, my shin, the lack of sleep, the river. The trail is as unrelenting as the rain was earlier today.

After the river, we had to cross a steep snowfield. The trail was buried by crusty ice, and the mountainside plunged into a precipitous oblivion below. I punched my poles into the snow and prayed the grip on my shoes would hold me to the ground as I inched across the slope.

After the snowfield, the trail wound through piles of jagged volcanic debris. The dirt path disappeared into mounds of rocks and we kept losing the trail. Spinning circles around the night searching for hints of a path in the rubble. Every unnecessary step off trail was insult to injury, salt in the wound.

Now we're on the final descent to the trailhead where Ian should be parked. But this hill is unending and every step is a battle.

It's 3:30 A.M. and I am falling asleep while shuffling down the trail. My steps are the voices that keep jolting me awake.

I thought my shin was bad earlier, but it's nothing compared to the searing pain I'm wading through now. The trail is covered in small rocks, and every whisper of contact with a pebble is met with a howl from my leg.

I curse as my foot hits the ground. An especially painful step unleashes an anguished "fuck" into the night. The rawest part of me is fighting for every step forward.

I squint my eyes and watch each foot hit the ground beneath the beam of my headlamp. I've been doing this for over twenty hours. I can't believe how hard today got, how the immensity of it has felt impossible to overcome. I've doubted my ability to get through this day from the moment I started running this morning. To get through the next step. It didn't make sense that I could persist through such excruciating conditions. That I could keep going through so much pain and fatigue and misery. Especially as it kept getting worse and worse.

I think back to the morning I woke up after my mother's death. No part of me could have seen myself running across Oregon on that day. I didn't understand how I could ever do anything but blink my eyes through so much pain.

I stumble through another step and look up. The beam of my headlamp follows my gaze. Finally, I see the dark silhouette of the van. I drop my eyes back down to my feet and watch myself take the final steps through the black night.

ABOVE: Picking up bibs for the 2010 Vermont City Marathon (VCM) with my brother and mom. RIGHT: Visiting covered bridges (one of my mom's favorite things) in Oregon with my mom and Brutus. BELOW: Jess and Jameson on their wedding day in Shelburne, Vermont. August 25, 2018.

ABOVE: Nearing the finish of VCM with my mom.

BELOW: Hanging out with my best friend, Brutus, on the Oregon coast.

TOP: After my mom lost her hair to chemotherapy, she road-tripped to Maine with her girlfriends to attend a diner's Bald Thursday, where she got a discount on her coffee and breakfast. CENTER: Spending time in Vermont with my mom. BOTTOM: Running on the bike path along Lake Champlain while my mom biked ahead of me. I'd flown back to Vermont to see her after we learned her chemotherapy didn't work.

ABOVE: At the California-Oregon border with Ian and Dilly, moments before starting to run on August 1, 2020. *Photo by Jon Meyers.* BELOW: Signing the trail register at the California-Oregon border. *Photo by Jon Meyers.*

ABOVE: Running through sunrise on my first day, feeling both overwhelmed by the miles ahead and grateful to be on the trail. BELOW: Getting to my first crew stop on my second day of running, with Dilly Pickle Chip excitedly escorting me through my last few steps to the van. *Photo by Jon Meyers.*

ABOVE: A snapshot of gear at a crew stop on Wahtum Lake. BELOW: Heading into the night with Danielle pacing me.

A typical night on the PCT, eating macaroni and cheese in bed while snuggling Dilly.

Hitting the 200-mile mark and feeling a lot of excitement about it.

ABOVE: Running past Rosary Lakes, a little before reaching the halfway point on the trail. BELOW: Getting some lakeside physical therapy from Joe Uhan. My body was in pretty good shape at this point, but (spoiler alert) that was about to change.

ABOVE: Hanging out with friends on Charlton Lake, on the one night I finished before sunset. My Tuesday night running group showed up in a big way to help make my fourth day an incredibly fun and joyful one. RIGHT: Running through meadows of lupine on my fifth day, while Alli and Riggs paced me through the Three Sisters Wilderness.

The trail traveled past three of the biggest and most stunning
volcanoes in Oregon during my fifth day.

RIGHT: Moving toward McKenzie Pass, as the weather starts to shift. BELOW: The weather took a turn for the worse on my sixth day on the trail.

RIGHT: Trying to psych myself up to head back out into the storm after my crew stop at Santiam Pass. It would be several hours and about 30 miles before I would see my crew, or dry clothes, again. BELOW: Running through the brutal storm with Eric

Eric sent Ian an honest, and accurate, satellite message during the storm. It was, in fact, a very long night.

Warming up and taking a nap before heading back into the night after running through the storm all day. Leaving this sleeping bag was one of the hardest things I did on the trail.

ABOVE: Getting fed a quesadilla by Nick and Ian while Callie worked on my shin at an especially cheerful crew stop near Mount Hood. I was absolutely spoiled with support during this run from many amazing friends. BELOW: Asking my crew if I'd made it to the "final push" on my last day on the trail. They enthusiastically told me, "Hell yes." *Photo by Jon Meyers.*

ABOVE: Celebrating on the Bridge of the Gods after setting a new overall record on the Oregon PCT in 7 days, 19 hours, and 23 minutes. *Photo by Jon Meyers.* BELOW: Hugging Danielle Snyder on the Bridge of the Gods. Danielle established the women's record on the Oregon PCT in 2019. *Photo by Jon Meyers.*

Feeling every emotion after reaching the Oregon-Washington
border, with Ian and Dilly. *Photo by Jon Meyers.*

Seven

RUNNING IS A LOVE LANGUAGE

AUGUST 7, 2020
DAY SEVEN—BREITENBUSH LAKE TO MOUNT HOOD
54.7 MILES, 5,719 FEET OF CLIMBING

November 2019

Two months before I lost my mom, I stood beside the crater she would leave behind and stared over the edge.

It was late November, after her health had taken a nosedive. She was still in the clinical trial but she'd rapidly lost her ability to do anything but lie on the couch, looking out the window at the bleak Vermont landscape.

Her spirits spiraled as rapidly as her physical health. She responded to texts with one-word answers—if at all. She avoided phone calls. Her friends took her on a drive to get her out of the house, but it just made her feel worse, as she confronted the chasm between the life she had loved and the threadbare days she was left with.

"You should come home as soon as you can," my aunt Mary told me over the phone on a Sunday evening. I was climbing in Southern Oregon when she called. I watched my friend crest the towering rock wall as the yolky sun dripped into the cracks of the cliffs.

I booked a flight for the week after Thanksgiving and got a ticket for Ian. I wanted him there with me, but more than that, I wanted him to meet my mom while he still could.

A few days before we left, we went to a wedding at an old hotel outside Portland. The couple getting married were friends of Ian's. I was there as a plus one, floating on the outskirts of the evening.

We wandered the grounds before the ceremony started with pints of beer in hand. I walked through the cold grass, detached from the pomp of the event around me. I'm not much of a wedding person. I've spent exactly zero minutes imagining my own wedding. I don't have opinions about cuts of diamonds or floral arrangements. And I've always known if and when I get married, it will be a casual affair. No white dresses or first dances. Weddings don't stir up many emotions from me. At least they didn't used to.

When it was time to sit down for dinner, we found our table, which was full of Ian's housemates and their dates. The ballroom hummed with loud conversation and clanking silverware. The noise faded as the bride's father walked up to the front of the room and turned a microphone on. He paused and flashed an adoring smile at his daughter.

He started sharing a story about her. The bride beamed as her father looked at her with radiant love. My breath caught in my throat. A wave of tears surged through me. I bit the inside of my lip, trying to hold them down, afraid of what would happen if they broke through the dam I was building. The ballroom erupted in laughter as he kept talking. I closed my eyes and sucked in my breath. I felt a tear crest my eyelid.

I grabbed a maroon napkin and slipped it to the corner of my eye, trying to hide the fact that I was on the brink of a meltdown.

The bride's father raised a champagne glass in the air. I looked into my lap. A wall of tears pressed my eyes like a battering ram against a door. I tried to numb out the voices speaking in the background. I couldn't bear to hear one more word of unconditional parental love.

My breaths grew more panicked as I thought about all the things that my mother would miss. My wedding. Decades of birthdays and holidays. A first book. Every big run I attempted and finished. Everything my mother would never dream of missing. Everything I couldn't imagine doing without her. Everything I always assumed she would be there for. The same woman who sat in the bleachers for ten straight hours at every swim meet, with a highlighted program on her lap so she could watch me swim for thirty-seven seconds, would be first in line to buy my book.

I stood up and walked as fast as I could toward the bathroom. I couldn't hold it in for another second. The crater was all I could see—and I didn't know how I could live, swallowed by such empty darkness.

Mile 361,
Mount Hood National Forest

Yesterday was the most miserable run of my life.

But today feels even worse.

My heart sinks to the pit of my stomach as soon as I blink my eyes open. *I don't know if I can keep going.*

When I set out to do this run, I had the same conversation with my crew that I've had before every big run: my threshold for quitting.

I am not a runner who subscribes to the mentality of "death before DNF," the oft-dreaded acronym for Did Not Finish. I believe there are many good reasons to quit a run and have pulled the plug on plenty. I dropped out of a 50k on Orcas Island because the last six-mile descent was better suited for mud wrestling than running and I didn't want to risk falling as I was just coming back from a strained hip.

But on this run, with every step celebrating my mom's life, and raising money for rare cancer research through the Brave Like Gabe Foundation, I don't want to quit for anything but serious injury—or worse.

"Don't let me stop unless I have a broken bone," I told Ian as we were driving down to the Siskiyous to start the run. The van was swaying like a carnival ride as he maneuvered the potholes and rocks that covered the dirt road.

"Scratch that," I said. "Certain broken bones would be okay. If it's just a nose or finger, I want to keep going. If I can't walk, you can let me quit."

When I wake up to a throbbing shin, I wonder how close I am to my breaking point. I think back to last night, when every step against the ground was met with excruciating pain.

I know I am tangoing with a serious injury right now. I'm terrified I'm already there.

As miserable as yesterday was, there's nothing I want more than to run fifty-five miles today. I'm here to honor my mom, and I will absolutely walk barefoot across burning coals to do that.

I pick up my phone and flick the screen on. I see an "X" where bars of service should be. I let out a frustrated sigh. I want to text Joe, my physical therapist, to ask him what I should do before I commit to any decisions. I trust him to give me an honest assessment of the consequences that I'm risking if I keep going.

I peer out the van's window and see the sun burning in the sky. I look at my phone again. It's already 8:30 A.M. I need to get moving soon if I'm going to start this day. I have fifty-five miles to cover, and I can't afford to adjust the stopping point again. Not if I want a shot at this record.

I slide off the bed and stumble over to my pile of running clothes. I decide I want to at least keep going until I have cell service. Until I can ask Joe what I should do, what I may risk if I press on.

I ease my body out of the van and step into the swampy summer air. Eric walks over from behind his truck. He's limping as he shuffles toward me, not from injury, but from twenty-two-and-a-half hours of running through the night. I recognize the steps he's taking. It's the gait of running to the edge.

I know I must look even more battered than he does.

He's in a pair of jeans and a T-shirt. He nods at my running clothes with an impressed smile.

"You're ready to go," he says.

"Trying," I say back.

"This is how records are won," he says with a glimmer in his eye. His smile grows wider. I remember him telling me the same thing last night. When no part of me wanted to keep going.

Today, it's all I want to do.

January 2020
Vermont

On the other side of my mother's death, Vermont turned into the worst alternate universe. Everything looked the same as it always had. The place

I'd known for thirty-five years was embedded in my veins, but it was immediately different in the most haunting way. My mother had been an integral part of every way I'd known Vermont, and I couldn't so much as drive past the gas station without seeing her walk out with a hazelnut coffee in hand. Memories of my mom followed my every movement. Her absence stuck with me like a shadow.

I went to my parents' house before I flew back to Oregon so I could look through some of my mother's things and bring a few of the more sentimental items home with me. I walked upstairs to her bedroom and opened the drawer in the lefthand corner of her big oak dresser. I knew my mom wanted me to have her wedding ring, along with one from each of my grandmothers. She'd put all three in a small white box with my name etched into the top. I went to look for it in the places I assumed it would be: the back corner of her sock drawer, her maroon jewelry box on the dresser, her bedside table.

I started with the sock drawer. I slid my hand into the back corner and ran it along the edge, but there was nothing but solid wood and balled-up socks. I opened the jewelry box next, but there were no rings inside. I walked over to the bedside table and pulled out the small drawer. But found nothing but books and a small reading light.

I started tearing through every drawer and shelf in her room. I shoved my hand into the same corner of the sock drawer dozens of times. I ripped apart pairs of socks and threw them on the floor. But there was no sign of the rings anywhere I looked.

Panic churned inside of me. Not because I couldn't find the rings, but because I couldn't ask my mom where they were. She was the only person in the world who knew where to find those rings.

I collapsed onto the floor. I thought of all the questions I'd never asked her, and all of the stories and memories that vanished with her. So many pieces of her life only existed with her, and now, they had died, too. I would never be able to ask my mom anything ever again. I wept, for everything I had lost alongside my mother, for everything I would keep losing.

Mile 364,
Mount Hood National Forest

As Ian and I start running, we're on the hunt for two things: Cell service. And Eli.

Eli is supposed to run most of today with me, but we have no idea where he is.

The original plan was to meet him at Olallie Lake, where I was going to sleep last night. But when we revised the mileage plan on Woodpecker Ridge, Eli must've already been out of service and Ian couldn't get a message to him. We suspect he went to the trailhead I'd intended to make it to—but Ian tried to find him there in the middle of the night and saw no sign of his truck.

There's a chance we'll find him in five miles—and there's a chance he's out on his own wild goose chase, trying to track us down because we didn't show up last night or early this morning.

We run in and out of the shadows of lodgepole pines and it feels like we're stuck in an SAT problem as we go. "If Eli slept at Olallie Lake and we didn't show up by 9:00 A.M., would he run five miles up the trail or drive two hours to the next trailhead?"

My brain is an anxious mess. My shin is a flashing "check engine" light. And my MIA pacer is the black cloud growing on the horizon.

The trail grinds uphill and my quads burn with the climb. The bright sun bakes my skin. Beads of sweat pool on my bare shoulders.

I think back to twenty-four hours ago. When I could feel the icy rain in my bones and violent gusts of wind threatened to whip me off a ridgeline. The harsh sun overhead makes the storm feel like another lifetime. But my body reassures me it wasn't. Every step today is through the hangover of that storm.

My shin pounds as I run—and the only thing as loud as the pain is my stress about whether I can keep going.

Ian runs with his phone in his hand, checking every few steps to see if we've climbed high enough to find a signal.

"Do we have service yet?" becomes my constant refrain. I'm an impatient child in the back seat on a road trip.

Finally, Ian yelps with relief at the sight of a bar of service. It's not enough to make a phone call so we stop in the middle of the trail to text Joe—and wait for his response. I'm nervous we'll lose service again if we take another step. So, we linger beneath the shade of a tree and hope that Joe responds soon.

My pulse races as I wait for the phone to vibrate. But I don't have to wait long at all. Joe texts back in less than a minute.

"How bad is it?" he asks.

"Do you have tape?" is his next question.

I grab the phone from Ian and frantically fill him in on the status of my shin.

"It hurts every step," I text. "It's some of the worst pain I've ever run through."

"Try not to stress too much," he texts back. "You should be able to keep going."

He promises he'll see me in a few miles and reassures me that it might hurt, but it's okay to run on it. He sends pictures to Ian, with instructions about how to tape it for stability and adds a few words that could definitely go on a locker room poster about how pain is temporary and glory is forever.

With Joe's blessing, I feel better about moving forward, even if every step is a battle.

I start running again. The pain is blinding.

I think about something I've heard professional runner Lauren Fleshman say about running: "To choose your method of suffering is a privilege."

With grief and pain both coursing through my body, with so much senseless loss and sickness in my family, with an awareness of those who are not able to choose their suffering, I am flooded with gratitude that I get to choose to keep going through this kind of pain.

January 2020
Eugene, Oregon

There's a heavy fog clouding a lot of my memories from the days and weeks after my mom died.

I can't remember flying back to Oregon. I don't know if I landed in Eugene or Portland. Or if Ian and I were on the same flight. I can't remember going back to work. If I took a few days off or plunged back in. If I had uncomfortable conversations with coworkers or if I cried in the bathroom on my first day back.

My grief felt like the eye of a hurricane. An eerie quiet surrounded by raging storms. I'd spent months drowning in the anxiety of my mom's cancer. I'd lived on the razor's edge of her death. My waking moments were flooded with fear, and I self-medicated with gummies from the dispensary down the street to get any sleep.

On the other side of her death, that constant hum of anxiety was replaced by the white noise of life without her. I sensed the ways that her absence would destroy me. That the hole in my heart would never fill back in. But in the initial aftermath of her death, I felt disoriented. Unmoored. A lost child.

Those weeks and months after her death are full of blank space in my memory. Like my brain couldn't compute a life without my mom.

But a thing I do remember is that one of the first runs I went on was a disaster.

I was back in Oregon and knew I needed to get outside.

I headed out behind my house and took the shortcut through the schoolyard to get to the closest trailhead. The trail pitched up and the trees shot to the sky. I climbed the hill and my breath got shorter and faster.

I thought of the first run I took my mom on in Eugene. She'd visited less than a month after I moved here, because she wanted to immediately see my new home. She liked to be able to picture the everyday parts of my life: my house, my reading nook, my desk, my commute to work, my running routes. She wanted to be able to see and feel the texture of my life. If I called her during a walk around my neighborhood, she wanted to be able to put herself there with me, imagining each apple tree and rosebush I strode past.

During that trip, we ran on the path that meanders along the banks of the Willamette River. I'd run on this trail every time I visited Eugene and knew it would see many of my miles in my new town. She stopped on the bridge to take a picture of the rapids below and wrapped her arm around me.

"When I'm running along the river in Lincoln, I'll think of you running along your river in Eugene," she said.

I pictured the New Haven River that snaked through the town of Lincoln, Vermont. My mom's footsteps along it had felt as reliable as the current that runs from the Green Mountains to the valley below. And now her steps had just vanished. She would never run along that river again.

I heard my own footsteps hitting the soft dirt beneath me. My breath quickened, even as the trail flattened out. My inhalations hit a logjam in my throat. Panic expanded across my airway and my breaths had nowhere to go.

I collapsed into a tree, gasping for air.

I slid to the ground and wrapped my hands behind my head, elbows wide, trying to reclaim my breath from the panic attack that stopped me in my tracks.

I heaved. I'd barely made it a mile. It felt like I would never be able to run again.

Mile 366,
Mount Jefferson Wilderness

I run beneath the burning sun and the pain sends shock waves through me.

I try to settle into it. To accept the sensation. It's not going anywhere anytime soon. And I need to find a way to run through it for the next fifty miles, to run with it.

I try to think about other times I've pushed past what made sense in an effort to reassure myself that I can get through this. It's a mental trick I use to persist through my lowest lows on my hardest runs. I remind myself that if I've done X hard thing, then I can do this hard thing.

I don't have to dig deep into my memory to remember other times when it's felt impossible to keep running.

But I've never been here before. With such immense pain and so many steps to go.

I know I'm going to need more than a few mental tricks to get through today.

August 2019
Lincoln, Vermont

The month before my mom started her clinical trial, she asked for help in the most Andrea Halnon way.

She was feeling scared and overwhelmed, so she posted a request on Instagram for her friends, family, and online running and triathlon community.

"I need a distraction," she said. "I want to remind cancer that I'm a badass who's still fighting hard—will you 'give' me miles this week from your own runs, bikes, swims, or canoes? My goal is to get 500 miles of support by the end of the week."

She wanted to fill her dance card with walking partners again, but this time, in a more symbolic way that allowed people around the world to join her.

I went to the Oregon coast that week to meet Ian's family, who had flown out to stay in a house on a rocky bluff, with sweeping windows that gazed out on the rolling tides.

I ran on the beach the afternoon I got there, feet sinking into the sand. I remembered visiting the coast with my mom during her last trip to Oregon. We'd found a trail down to the beach through the grassy dunes and walked for miles with Brutus chasing seagulls and frothy waves.

I texted my mom a photo from the run, with the sea rippling behind me.

"These miles are for you," I told her. "I wish you were here, by the ocean, with me. I thought about you the whole way."

I asked my running friends from the Tuesday night Hunt to share their miles, too. "Could you send my mom a text this week with a photo from your run? And let her know you're thinking of her and sending her your miles for support."

My running friends delivered. They shared selfies from runs around Eugene and out in the Cascade foothills. They recruited their family members to join. Daniel's and Andrew's parents went for a hike on the McKenzie River together and sent her a beaming group selfie beside the opal water. Ashley and Daniel snapped a photo with their baby, Miles, and dog, Disco, and sent it to my mom.

She hit her 500-mile goal by the second day. People from Iowa to South Africa to Australia shared 519 miles with her that day alone.

My mom posted an update about her miles every day, along with a report from her own outings. Bike rides by covered bridges and lighthouses. She racked up hundreds of miles each day, from people around the world. By the end of a week, she had 2,574 miles from twenty-five states and ten countries. You could see her spirits lift with each text and mile. At the beginning of the week, she'd been overwhelmed by the looming clinical trial. And by the end, she was ready to weather the next challenge, feeling held by everyone who loved and supported her.

"This was the most heartwarming week," she said at the end of the seven days. "It was exactly what I needed."

Mile 366,
Mount Hood National Forest

We're about to hit five miles when I see the best thing ahead of us on the trail. There's a person jumping up and down and there's no question it's Eli.

He's easy to spot, in his hot pink shorts and bright cobalt shirt. He's reliably the best-dressed athlete on the trails. He doesn't go anywhere without his trusty bin full of sequin gowns, floral sundresses, and rainbow tutus.

He's also hard to miss because he's usually operating at a volume turned up to eleven. He once speculated that he never sees wildlife on the trail because he scares them away with his constant stream of chatter and yelps. Which is believable as he greets us with enough decibels to fill a football stadium.

"EMILY! YOU'RE A QUEEN!" Eli hollers, limbs flailing in every direction.

I bounce up to him and wrap him in a tight hug.

"I'm so happy to see you here!" I say, wiggling my body against his as I hug him.

"Eli! Me too," Ian says and lets out a sigh of relief. He fills Eli in on how he biked miles to the trailhead at 4:00 A.M., looking for him and his truck.

"I was parked just past the sign!" Eli cries. "You must have missed me by inches."

Ian drops his face into his palms and shakes it back and forth. "I can't believe how close I was," he says.

"I'm so glad I found you," Eli says. "I was so worried Emily had to evacuate off the trail during the storm yesterday."

Ian throws his arms around Eli in a big hug. "I'm just glad you're here and we found you. I'll see you two in a few hours," he says.

Ian blows me a kiss and yells out, "You're doing it, babe," as he runs off the trail.

Eli and I start jogging north. His brightness—in looks and spirit—gives me a much-needed burst of energy. Eli is the perfect elixir after yesterday's storm, while I'm fighting to get through every step. He's been through some serious shit with me on—and off—the trail.

He was running with me when I snapped the bone in my wrist in the middle of the twenty-mile loop around Three Fingered Jack on the Fourth of July. We had to hike miles out with my arm in the air like a sad flagpole. I went into shock from the pain right after I fell, and Eli held me upright so I didn't fall into a pile of my own waste as my body expunged the shock of the broken bone.

Eli also lived with me for all thirteen months of my mom's cancer. He's been one of my first hugs during many breakdowns. He's cooked me dinner when I could barely get off the couch. And he's run with me through it all.

He is the perfect friend to pace me through most of today, while I'm weathering the worst pain and fatigue of any run I've ever been on.

"What do you think Robyn would wear if she were running with us now?" Eli asks me. He's shaking his hips a little as he trots down the trail in front of me.

He doesn't wait for me to respond before he shouts out his thoughts on the matter.

"I think she'd be in a sequined bodysuit. And she'd be a smart queen and apply enough body glide to avoid chafing. And matching thigh-high boots!" he shrieks.

This is one of our favorite games to play on the trail together. "Which diva would be the best running partner on this climb?" "What do you think Mariah Carey would put in her hydration pack?" "Could Taylor's red lipstick go the distance on the trail?"

It's a much-needed distraction from the stress I've been drowning in all morning. I watch Eli run and imagine Robyn trying to keep up with us in sequined thigh-high boots.

The land around us is brown and crisp. The summer air is piping hot and dry. It's like inhaling the desert. I remember Danielle saying this portion of the trail was one of her hardest parts, as the terrain rolled into a monotonous stretch of hot and exposed miles. It's believable she felt that way, as we run through the arid ground.

"Do you think Celine was referring to running across Oregon when she sang about endless pleasure?" Eli asks, as he flicks sweat off his forehead.

"What else could she possibly mean?" I shout back, as I heave my body over a dead tree fallen across the trail. The abrasive bark scratches my flesh as I straddle the log. I land on my bad shin and pain courses through me.

2011
Vermont

My mom set running goals every year. They were always composed in her teacherly manner, a tidy list, color-coded and organized by categories. It brought me back to childhood summers, where we would scrapbook our way through family vacations and educational field trips around Vermont. She loved to have us fill pages with our favorite displays from museums or our vote for the best beach in Maine.

Her goals could fill a scrapbook of their own with their very Andrea Halnon nature—"run in three new states," "race in two new counties in Vermont," and "race every calendar month."

And she always included a goal about running with her family and friends.

"My favorite thing is to run with my family as much as I can," she said every January.

I was an easy sell to help her with this one, especially when I still lived in Vermont. She recruited me to help her check off all kinds of boxes from her list, at races near and far. My mom went to great lengths to meet certain goals. Like when she ran a 5k in two left shoes because she wanted to cross a new Vermont county off her list and had driven hours to do it, unknowingly leaving the right footwear behind. And she convinced me to follow suit and go to ridiculous measures to help her. We'd road-trip hours around New England to race in a new state or hit one of the tougher calendar months.

We once drove to New Hampshire on a cold January weekend to run the Inauguration Day 5k, when Barack Obama was sworn into office. It was below zero, and I could see my breath puffing into the air as we picked up our bibs. We huddled in the car before the start, blasting heat and The Chicks, avoiding the freezing temperatures outside until we absolutely had to go run. I ran in my black puffy jacket, zipped over a fleece coat and long-sleeve shirt. And crossed the finish line with a red nose and numb toes.

When we were done running, we raced back to the car and cranked the heat. We drove back to Vermont with our matching race shirts and gas station hot cocoas. We'd traveled four hours, each way, to run for just over twenty minutes in subarctic conditions.

When my brother decided to run his first marathon at the Vermont City Marathon, my mom asked me if I would do the race with her as a relay. It was the same race she'd done as her first marathon and one she still loved to be at every May.

I flew up from DC for the weekend. It was her dream. All three of us sharing the same race. We went to the expo together to pick up our bibs. My mom walked over to the course map and told Jameson where her favorite spots were along the marathon.

Jameson and I ran the first half together. She was waiting on Church Street and burst into excited cheers when she saw us. When I got to the halfway point, she jumped in with me to run her half marathon. I was running the full thing but got to count my first half toward our relay. We ran the rest of the race together and finished arm in arm.

"I got to race with both of my babies today," she said, as we walked through the grassy field beside Lake Champlain after we all finished. She was bouncing with glee as we made our way through the crowd. She hugged us both and said, "That was one of my happiest days."

Running was my mom's favorite love language.

Mile 381,
Mount Hood National Forest

We hear our friends before we see them.

We are running through a forest thick with giant fir trees. The raucous cheers and cowbell clanks float through the woods. My stride responds and I bound into the intersection.

Whenever I've raced a 100-miler, my friends who are crewing and pacing me want to know how they can best help me. They expect me to give them a detailed list about the ounces of hydration mix I need in my soft flasks and the specific socks I want swapped at precise mile marks. But I always tell them the same thing.

"Just be at the aid stations," I say. "You have no idea how much of a boost I get from seeing friends for a few minutes."

It's not unlike how much support my mom found through her walking, running, and biking friends. I count down the miles and steps until I can get another round of hugs and high fives. They're the carrot reeling me along through my hardest miles.

At Cascade Crest last summer, my friends were at each aid station with a boombox and piles of flair. When I got to mile twenty-nine, they were dancing to Sofi Tukker in tutus and sparkly crop tops, and I jumped in with them, shaking my hips and throwing my arms up to the sky. A volunteer came over and told me to "get the hell out of here" so I didn't waste too much time at the aid station, when I had seventy-one miles of racing left to do.

A similar sight greets me when I run into the crew stop.

The crew has swelled in numbers—and volume—since this morning. A large group of my Eugene friends has shown up and they are decked in head-to-toe flair. The trailhead is a gyrating wall of sequins, feathers, and metallic silver. A speaker blares Kesha. The group is swaying with the beat and bellowing cheers as I run into the parking area.

I hear my name from a dozen different directions as I slow down and come to a stop.

Joe immediately pulls me over to his table to check out my shin.

I stretch out across the deep blue cushion, lying face toward the sky. He yanks off my shoddy tape job and digs into my shin.

"How does this feel?" he asks. He prods different spots on my lower leg as he asks me questions about the pain.

"Every step hurts," I say.

I point to the source of the most excruciating pain and he nods as he continues to dig into my muscles.

He works on it and retapes it, in a much sleeker-looking configuration of medical tape.

He shows me how to work on it on the trail—kneading the softest part of my upper shin.

"You can dig into this muscle up here," he says. "It should help take some of the pressure off of your tendon. It's not going to get rid of all the pain, but you should be able to keep going and finish."

I nod, biting back tears. The idea of running another eighty-some miles through such horrendous pain is overwhelming.

My friend Nick dances over in a child's-sized sloth apron, holding a big pot of ramen.

"Did someone order some noodles?" he says in a singsong pitch. Eli and Stacy are twerking beside the table. Stacy's long dark ponytail bounces with her hips.

This energy is exactly what I needed. Rowdy, loud, colorful merriment to balance out the dark festering stress I've felt all morning. And the dread I'm feeling about moving through the pain for another day and a half.

I take grateful bites of steaming ramen. I change out my socks and shoes after Joe is done working on my shin. I take a deep breath. I have another twenty miles to go today. The pain is a lot, but I get to keep going. All I want to do is keep going.

When I am ready to go, my friends send me off with another fast-paced pop song. Every hand is in the air, waving me into the woods.

I follow Eli, Nick, and a few other friends down the trail as it weaves through the forest.

The rowdy energy from the trailhead stays with us as we start running. I let Eli carry the conversation as I settle into my stride.

I think about how one of the things that made it easier to be away from my mom while she was sick was knowing she was surrounded by a circle of women who would do anything to support her. They made her meals. They went with her to chemotherapy appointments. They drove to Boston to sit with her through her clinical trial. They walked and biked with her. And they sent her an endless stream of cards and texts to make sure she never forgot that she was surrounded by love and support.

As I follow my chattering friends, I know she'd feel the same about me on this run. She would be so stressed about all that could go wrong. But she would be so comforted by how incredibly supported I am out here. If she was following the run from Vermont, she'd look at a photo from my crew at Timothy Lake and breathe a little easier.

February 2020
Eugene, Oregon

I had to start training for my PCT run as soon as I got back to Oregon from my mom's funeral in Vermont. The only problem was that I could barely get myself out the door.

When I picked my start date for the PCT, the beginning of August stood out as the most strategic choice. It was ideal timing for snowmelt, bugs, and wildfire. The trails would have time to dry out beneath the deep snowpack from winter. The notorious mosquitoes that swarm the Cascades as the snow melts would die down. And I should be able to beat the wildfires that can rage across the West every summer—and the choking smoke that accompanies them.

But when I counted backward from my rough start date in August, I realized I needed to start training right away. I could barely remember to brush my teeth in the morning, but I was going to have to find a way to prepare for a 460-mile run across the state of Oregon.

For my first long run, I planned to do a sixteen-mile loop around the trails behind my house. I tied my shoelaces like my fingers were dragging through molasses. I walked out the door, each step feeling like my legs were wading through shin-deep water. I felt the magnetic pull of my bed trying to hold me back.

I started running uphill toward the Blanton Trailhead. The sky was the chalky gray of Oregon winter. My insides had been stained gray for weeks. Soft raindrops started to fall. I thought about my mom, running through every dip of a Vermont winter. Walking every day through chemotherapy. Her hood pulled over her head when the temperatures dropped below zero. I saw her beaming after those walks.

The road met the trail and the soft ground held me as I ran uphill. I felt the memories of my mom cradle me as I ran.

I thought about when long runs became a ritual for me. I remember training for my first marathon after my mom inspired me to run one. She was so excited to support me. She wanted to hear every detail about my runs, where I went, how many miles I did, if I ate gels or gummies, if I drank enough water, what my favorite part of the route was. One weekend, I ran eighteen miles from my apartment in Burlington to my parents' house in Lincoln. My mom was waiting at the end of their long driveway with a cold Coke and a bag of snacks and then drove me the forty-five minutes back home, peppering me with questions the entire way and telling me stories about training for her first marathon.

Running had been our love language since we ran that first marathon together, a thread woven through countless texts, phone calls, conversations, and memories. And as I kept running down the trail, I could feel that it still was.

My mom is what got me out the door during the rawest and hardest days of grief. As I flailed in the world without her, I found her on my runs. When I needed my mom more than ever before, she was there to help me keep running.

Mile 401,
Mount Hood National Forest

The sun is a clementine, sinking deep into the sky. It slips between the trees and darkness swoops down on the forest.

I let my friends chatter away and escape into the silence. I'm too tired to join, but the hum of conversation is solace. I feel surrounded by support, but it gives me enough space to run with my mom close. Every step today has felt charged by my love for her.

The trail rolls gently uphill, as it begins the long ascent up Mount Hood, the last Cascade in the chain of volcanos across Oregon. I look down at my legs and am surprised by how well I'm moving. I'm running with a sense of ease through the labor of the climb.

I remember how hard it was to shuffle through the final steps of yesterday. How it felt like the day would never end because each step had to battle a millennium of time and a world of pain. How scared I was that I would have to quit.

Tonight, I'm still tired and in pain, but I found what I needed to get through this day. I held onto my mom through every breath and every step.

May 2006
Lincoln, Vermont

When my mom ran her first marathon, she dedicated each of her final six miles to someone special in her life. The idea was that each person would help her get through the hardest part of the race. She picked people who inspired her, like my aunt Mary, who had survived breast cancer. And friends and family who had gone out of their way to support her through marathon training.

"And the last mile is for you, Jameson, and Dad," she said. "I know I won't quit on you."

Mile 405,
Mount Hood National Forest

The stars are fireflies in the sky. They burn bright through the black night.

I peer into the forest and see the faint glow of a headlamp through the trees ahead. I know I am about to pop out at the final trailhead of the day, where Ian is parked for one last night of sleep along the trail. To finish this day means I have just one day left to get to the Gorge.

I look down at my wrist. My headlamp illuminates my mom's bracelet, the turquoise cord threaded through the silver emblem, stamped with the words "Stay Brave." It was part of a collection that she got herself while she was sick, with different mantras about strength and courage on each one. She even asked the company if she could make a custom one—and if she could cuss in it. They enthusiastically agreed and made her a bracelet that said, "Fuck Cancer."

The one I'm wearing is inspired by Gabe Grunewald, a professional track runner who passed away from a rare cancer just months before my mom did. She embodied many of the same qualities as my mom, especially a resolve to live with hope and joy through cancer. It was easy to understand why my mom was drawn to her story while she was sick. And as soon as I decided to do the run, I knew I also wanted to raise money for her Brave Like Gabe Foundation, which supports rare cancer research, to give others more treatment options than my mom and Gabe had.

I run my finger over the engraved words. Stay Brave.

I put this on as I left Eugene because I wanted my mom with me during this run. But as I take my final steps of the day, I know this bracelet isn't my only connection to her on this trail.

I know that if there's any place I can find my mom, it's in every step I run.

Eight

TO THE GORGE

AUGUST 8, 2020
DAY EIGHT—MOUNT HOOD TO THE BRIDGE OF THE GODS
59 MILES, 8,547 FEET OF CLIMBING

Mile 406,
Mount Hood National Forest

As I hike up Mount Hood, I feel how the run has whittled away all of my layers. I tried to defend my body with tape and Band-Aids, body glide and foam rollers, needles and matches, stretches and massages, but my defenses could only go so far against 400 miles in a week.

My feet are covered in blisters and bandages. My flesh is rubbed raw and red—beneath my hydration pack, where my shorts hit my skin, along the line of my sports bra. My shin still screams with nearly every step. The bottoms of my feet feel like someone pounded them with a mallet. My shoulders are sore and bruised from carrying a pack for over sixteen hours a day. My skin is gritty with dirt, salt, and dried sunscreen. My body is drained from running so many miles every day and sleeping just a few hours each night.

And my emotional state is just as weathered. I'm as tender as a beating heart. A turtle without its shell. A pipe on the cusp of bursting.

I'm not even a mile in before I can tell I'll be at a high risk of crying all day.

The sound of my brother's voice is the first thing to break me.

I call Jameson as I'm hiking up Mount Hood. Soft sunlight streams through the canopy of Douglas firs. The morning breeze rustles through pine needles. My communication with the outside world has been limited to a few texts for necessities throughout the week. But today, I feel pulled to talk to Jameson as soon as I'm on the trail.

The phone barely registers a ring before he picks up.

"Emmy!" his voice shakes.

I start crying.

"Jameson," I say. "I think I'm going to do it."

I look down the trail and pinch tears out of my eyes. I can hear him sniffing on the other side of the line. I know that in another world, if Jess weren't so sick, he would be here right now. I know he's exactly where he should be. And that for so many reasons, least of all this run, we wish his life looked much different.

"I've refreshed your tracker thousands of times a day," he says. "Mom would be out of her mind. She'd be so proud of you."

Tears pour down my face, leaving splatters on the dirt as I hike uphill. Jameson knows more than anyone else what this run means. And what our mother would be feeling right now. We're both lost in a world without her, but we know having each other is part of how we'll find our way. When the loss of my mom left me unmoored, my brother anchored me in family.

"I love you, Emily," Jameson says. "I'm so proud of you. And Mom is, too."

We hang up, but my brother stays with me as I climb. His voice, a touchstone for why I'm out here, pushing through 400 miles of exhaustion to reach the other side of Oregon. My stride is heavy with fatigue but propelled by determination to finish this run. I dig my poles into the dirt.

I feel as raw as can be, moving north for one more day. With nothing left to shield me from the trail, I feel the full weight of every step.

Winter 2020
Eugene, Oregon

I wanted to extricate myself from the grief of losing my mom.

The pain was sharp and merciless. Shards of glass in my lungs. A hot coal on my heart. A black hole wrenching me into unending darkness, without hope or answers.

But I knew there was no escape.

I knew any attempt to outrun my grief would be futile. I'd learned many times that I can't evade pain—and that trying to avoid it is its own purgatory. I knew it would linger, and fester, and grow, until I was forced to confront it. Like black mold in the basement. I knew that no matter how hard I tried to look away, it would lurk in the shadows until it could blind me.

I tried to dull the edges with pot gummies at night, an extra drink before bed, mindless scrolling on my phone when grief swooped in like a hawk. But I could feel that there was no antidote to maternal loss.

There is just time that weathers the grief into something more bearable. And turns it into a callus on your heart. It's never gone. Never fully healed. It becomes part of you. Like skin and bones, and the scars etched into you forever.

And in the immediate wake of my mother's death, all I could feel was the knife's edge cutting into me.

Mile 410,
Mount Hood National Forest

My eyes are dry and bloodshot. I rub them as I hike, and it feels like there are Brillo pads beneath my eyelids.

I couldn't sleep a single second last night. As soon as I stripped off my running clothes and crawled into bed, a charged energy coursed through me. I stared at the ceiling through the black night, doing math in my head.

Fifty-five miles to the Bridge of the Gods. If I start running by 5:00 A.M., *I have twenty-two hours to get there.*

If I finish before 3:00 A.M., *I can get the overall record.*

I could get the overall record. The thought drummed through me. It glowed with possibility.

I can do this. The idea was electrifying, a triple shot of caffeine. The excitement pulsed through my bloodstream and kept me awake, staring at the shadows of trees stretching up outside the van. I closed my eyes and tried to beckon sleep, but my brain couldn't stop racing toward the bridge.

It was always my goal to go for the overall record. To try to beat the men's times as well, both supported and self-supported. But it was a goal that felt outlandish. Almost too ridiculous to utter out loud. Almost too outrageous to even think to myself.

But there was a bold part of me, encouraged by the memory of my mother, that decided to go for it, despite my insecurities. That was the point of this run. I wanted to chase the biggest, scariest, and most exciting thing for her. The mark that pushed me to dig the deepest and to muster up the most courage. The goal that meant embracing the highest chance of failure and disappointment.

And as impossible as it felt, the part of me that is my mother's daughter allowed me to see the glimmer of possibility in the goal.

Today, that glimmer is a bolt of lightning.

I wrote out an Instagram post while I couldn't sleep. I've mostly been too tired and off-the-grid to touch social media this week, but I decided to put my biggest goal out there—and ask for support through the final push.

"I have fifty-five miles to go," I typed. "And I'm going for the *overall* record. Can you help me get there with donations to Brave Like Gabe?"

I posted it after I laced up my shoes and fastened my pack. My heart rate spiked with the double whammy of vulnerability. I was publicly sharing my most audacious goal—the one that felt too outlandish to name. And asking people to help me. I knew it was safer to do it this morning, when the goal seemed more achievable. But it still left me feeling exposed. Like I was posting my tender beating heart on the internet for anyone to poke and prod.

Now I can't stop looking at my phone. I've barely touched it all run, but the call to Jameson was just the start.

Eli and I are climbing through knee-high wildflowers as we get closer to the high point on Mount Hood. It's a scene straight out of *The Sound of Music*, but we're much dirtier and smellier than Maria.

We weave through a lush meadow as the dramatic summit comes into view. Dirty ribbons of snow fall down from it like tiger stripes, framing the jagged ledges of the volcano. After passing nine of Oregon's biggest Cascades, I can't believe this is the last one. I've covered the entire skyline of the state on foot in the last week.

I look at my phone again to see if I have service.

I'm antsy to check the donation page, which has been swelling with support since my post. And I'm itchy with the discomfort of sharing my greatest hopes for the run beyond my own head and heart. My palms are sweaty as I look at my phone. From the moment I shared my plans for this run, it's felt unnerving to open myself up to failure. But this is why I'm here.

I would rather fail going for the thing that sparks the biggest fire inside me than play it safe with a dream that's just an ember.

Winter 2020

There was one thought that comforted me in the immediate wake of losing my mom.

It didn't ease the grief; it didn't erase the pain. But it helped me see the loss through a different lens.

"You're hurting this much because of how immense your love with your mom was," a friend told me. She'd also lost her mom at a young age. She knew the kind of heartache I was living with.

I kept thinking about the truth of her words. They were a warm hug on my coldest days of grief.

I thought about how there was a direct correlation between love and grief. To feel grief was to feel love. They were in lockstep with each other.

The amount of pain I was feeling was eternally bound to how much love lived in my relationship with my mother. To how much love for her still lived in me.

I knew I wouldn't trade an ounce of that love for anything in the world.

Mile 430,
Mount Hood National Forest

I stand no chance against the emotional hurricane inside me when I get to my first big crew stop of the day.

The trail rolls downhill and opens up to a packed trailhead. Cars are parked all over the road. It's a jarring departure from the quiet trail.

I am relieved to spot Joe's big white van in the mess of cars. I know my shin is beyond any meaningful repair, but I trust Joe will give me temporary relief and a better tape job than the shoddy number I did this morning. The edges are frayed and crusted with dirt.

As I step off the trail, I feel like I am the tape. My own edges are frayed and weathered, leaving the most tender part of me exposed. I think back to Thursday's storm, when I was drowning in vulnerability. When everything felt like a threat.

Today's rawness feels different. I feel like a shell of myself. But I see how emptying myself out has helped me get here, to the last breath of Oregon. How the thing that leaves me feeling so ravaged is part of my strength.

I am surrounded by friends as soon as I set foot in the parking lot. Ian ushers me over to Joe's table with his hand on the small of my back.

"We brought you a burrito," he says. He hands me a white Styrofoam box with a burrito the size of my face inside.

I collapse onto Joe's table. My fatigued limbs surrender to gravity. It is bliss, to lie down and allow the core of the earth to draw my body deeper into a restful position. I close my eyes and fantasize about sleeping for a week straight.

Stacy covers me in a down blanket to keep me warm and loose. Joe starts digging his hands into my upper shin and Nicole feeds me bites of the breakfast burrito. Each greasy, salty bite of bacon and potato is ecstasy.

Ian walks around the table and kneels down so he can meet my eyes.

"Do you know how much the GoFundMe is up to?" he asks.

I nod. "At least close," I say. "I've been checking it all morning. It's incredible."

The response to my post was an immediate tidal wave of new donations—and they keep rolling in. The total has rocketed up thousands of dollars since this morning. It's over $25,000 now—and growing fast.

"Rachel asked people to share why they're donating," he tells me. "The stories are amazing. Do you want me to read some of them to you?"

My friend Rachel is a professional fundraiser, and she's been posting updates to my social media throughout the day from her home in Iowa. And asking people to share why they are giving to Brave Like Gabe.

I nod again. Not wanting to push the brink of my emotions or energy by doing anything more than that. I feel tears building and bite my lip to stop myself from flooding Joe's table.

Ian starts reading.

"Your mom inspired me to run my first 5k. This donation is to honor your badass mother and to give hope to others who are living with cancer."

"I lost my best friend and stepfather to this horrible disease. This donation is for them—and for your amazing mother and the beautiful memories she left us with."

"My mom was just diagnosed with a rare cancer and I'm giving this donation for her, and for Gabe Grunewald, and for your mom, and for you—for giving me hope."

"You are your mother's daughter. This donation is to cheer you all the way to the Bridge of the Gods."

There's no stopping it. I am a puddle on the table. The messages are so beautiful and devastating.

So many people feel inspired to give because they know a version of this pain. Or they see it looming on the horizon or know someone who has endured it. So many people have experienced the brutal and senseless loss caused by cancer—and want to create light that shines through the darkness of this disease. So many people are responding to this pain with love—and showing me how much love has survived the worst heartbreak, and how much empathy has grown from loss.

I wipe my eyes with the back of my hand and slide off the table. My body bucks the gravity that lulled into rest, for the greater force that's pulling me back to the PCT. There is no way I'm not making it to the Bridge of the Gods. I will crawl my way there if I need to.

March 2020
Eugene, Oregon

I didn't want to deal with another ounce of grief after my mother died, but I didn't have a choice when I had to say goodbye to Brutus just two months later.

It might sound ridiculous to compare the grief of losing my mom to the grief of losing a dog. To assert that they belong in remotely the same category of loss.

But I think about something the writer Nora McInerny said, after losing her father, husband, and unborn child in a matter of weeks, that there's no need to play the "bummer Olympics."

"This is not a competition to see whose troubles can beat up whose troubles. It's not a game of who has it worse. Nobody wants to win that game anyway."

Losing Brutus was its own inferno of grief. I didn't need to rank the severity of my losses to know that I was getting slapped with another earth-rupturing one. Saying goodbye to Brutus felt like a piece of me was ripped out forever. I could feel the haunting quiet of his absence in every corner of the house, in every corner of me.

I'd known I wouldn't be able to handle losing him since Brutus first burrowed his way into my heart and showed me how special it is to love and be loved by a dog. I'd known I could only stand to lose that love once in my lifetime.

Brutus was my first dog—and an unplanned foray into life with a canine best friend. I met Brutus through a relationship, and at the time I was indifferent to dogs—at best. When this guy told me he had a dog, my first thought was, *This is going to be annoying.*

But Brutus wasn't deterred by my lukewarm feelings about dogs and insisted on making himself my best friend. He napped at my feet while I was working, he bounded after me with his tail nub wagging when we stepped onto a trail, and he nuzzled his body into me at any hint of emotion.

On the eve of the 2016 election, I went to bed drunk and afraid that we were about to elect Donald Trump. I woke up in the middle of the night with excruciating back pain from a recent 100-miler and saw that my fears had been realized. I couldn't get back to sleep because my mental and physical state plummeted me into a doom spiral. I walked around the house shouting angry curses every few steps, lying on the floor and the couch. Unable to get comfortable and fall back asleep. Brutus followed me through every step and every wrench of my body, nuzzling into me and reminding me that he was there for me and he wasn't going anywhere. Every time I yelped out an angry "fuck," or let out an exasperated sigh when I couldn't get comfortable, he'd burrow his body deeper into mine. He always knew when I was in pain, and he met it with all of the love he could give.

By the time the relationship was on its last breath, I knew I was ready to be done with the guy—but not Brutus. So, I insisted on taking him with me. My ex had already started a new job in another state and left

Brutus behind when he went. I wasn't the first of his girlfriends whom he'd turned to for long-term dog care when Brutus became an inconvenience to him. And he didn't waste one word on pushing back when I said I wanted to keep Brutus forever. I think it was relief for him, to not feel held back by anyone or any dog. And Brutus deserved someone who saw him as the best life companion, not an inconvenience. I wanted nothing more than to be that someone. I found us a new dog-friendly place to live together in the south hills of town and vowed to give him the best golden years.

But, just as I hadn't expected to go through dog ownership, I wasn't prepared to go through the heartbreak of losing a dog. He was nearing ten when I fully embraced him as my own, but I was nowhere near ready to think about the end of his life.

"Brutus is an everlasting dog," I'd say. "He'll be my best friend forever."

The thought of ever living without Brutus by my side was too hot to touch. When he started to slow down as he got older, I refused to acknowledge what the signs of his aging meant.

But when the vet shone her flashlight into his mouth and saw that lump, I had to rapidly accept that he was going to die. And just a few weeks later, I had to say my last goodbye to Brutus. I crumbled as I watched his breaths fade to his final one, knowing I was doing the best thing for him, even if it felt like the worst thing for me.

The pain was even worse than the train wreck I was expecting. On my first night without him, I dropped to the floor of my bedroom and felt the deep incision of grief cutting into me again. The pain from losing my mother was still unbearable, and Brutus's death was a scalpel digging into a throbbing wound.

I never wanted to go through that pain again. I couldn't imagine deciding to get another dog and willingly subjecting myself to that much grief.

Mile 440,
Columbia River Gorge

I am running along a rocky ridge in the Columbia River Gorge and the uneven terrain is torture for my shin, for the pummeled soles of my feet, for my patience, which is worn as thin as the flesh on my heels.

I'm just twenty miles from the bridge, but it feels like the river is in Australia and I'm still in Oregon—a billion steps away from the end.

I want to see the contours of the bridge rising above the river in the next seven seconds. I want relief for my exhausted body, a magic carpet ride to the banks of the Columbia. I want painkillers made for a horse. But I know even livestock-grade ibuprofen wouldn't put a dent in what I'm feeling right now.

"Can I have Advil?" I ask Eli.

"Not for another two hours," he says. "But good news: it's time for more gummy bears!"

I roll my eyes and reluctantly stick out my palm for my mandatory calories. They feel as useless as the two dinky pills I'm swallowing every six hours. I know it's not safe, nor advisable, to take much ibuprofen while running, but that hasn't stopped me from fantasizing about robbing a pharmacy on my way to the bridge.

I think about how I'm out here to push my limits—to explore what I am capable of. I feel like I hit my limit at least five Cascades ago. And I'm still running. I am leaving every bit of me on this trail to get to the end.

I see my crew one last time at Wahtum Lake. There's an entire army of friends there to usher me through my final stop of the run.

"This is the last time we're doing this," Ian says as he wraps me in a big hug. "We'll see you at the bridge. You're almost there, babe." His voice is teeming with encouragement.

As I run away from my crew and the sandy campsite on Wahtum Lake, I don't feel almost there. The trail is a nasty descent. It's literally all downhill for miles, but nothing about it feels easy as the trail slices down a goliath rock canyon, with violent cliffs rising around us. It's steep and rocky and it doesn't give away a single step.

I think of the messages Ian read to me at Blodgett Pass. I think of everyone who has felt the deepest cut of grief and kept going. I think of my mom, running her first marathon. Pedaling along the bike path on Lake Champlain. Putting one foot in front of another through thirteen months of cancer.

I keep running through my flood of emotions. I keep running deep into the Gorge. I keep running toward my mom.

April 2020
Eugene, Oregon

The sight of dogs quickly felt like the older women who had triggered such intense feelings after my mom died.

I couldn't see one without feeling a storm of emotions. Anger. Grief. Longing.

"I never want to go through that again," I told my brother. "One and done. This is too much pain."

"I know you need time," my brother said. "But I hope you love another dog at some point in your life, because you have a lot of love to give. Brutus had the best life for the last four and a half years because he had you."

I thought about my years with Brutus. He'd introduced me to one of the most powerful types of love I'd ever known. He'd been my best friend and sidekick. I met Brutus right as I was starting therapy, and he was with me while I was learning how to heal parts of myself that I'd deemed unlovable. While I struggled to find love for myself, his love was unflinching.

While I was learning how to take care of myself, he brought out a nurturing side of me I didn't know I had. And he helped me be the most loving version of myself. Because I wanted nothing more than to give him the best life. When he got too old and gimpy to jump into the bed, I bought a new one that was low to the ground. When he couldn't hike as far, I found closer lakes to camp beside. We traveled fewer miles and played with more sticks. I modified the way I lived in his final years to accommodate an elderly schnauzer. I remember thinking it would be annoying to date someone with a dog, because it would mean skipping happy hours to let him out or planning vacations around dog-friendly destinations. But once I had Brutus in my life, I didn't think twice about wrapping my life around his and loving him in the biggest way I could. It was the only way I wanted to live.

As much as I couldn't imagine going through the torment of losing him again, I also knew my brother was right. I wanted that kind of love again. A dog's love is one of the most generous and meaningful kinds of love, and I knew that a life without it would have its own pain and emptiness.

I started looking at PetFinder in the middle of the night when I couldn't sleep. I didn't necessarily feel ready for another dog, but it was comforting to know that so many good dogs needed someone to love them and someone to love. When and if I was ever ready, I could have a dog in my life again.

Ian would wake up at 3:00 A.M. and see the neon glow of my phone next to him in bed. He'd look at the screen and see me zooming in on a rescue dog in Portland. I'd reach out my index finger and touch their button nose through the screen.

One morning, I saw a litter in Utah full of border collie–heeler mix puppies. I flipped through them, feeling a curious excitement about the litter. They were the first dogs I'd seen that I could imagine holding. That I could see running through my house. That I could feel my heart cracking open for.

I scrolled back and forth, oohing and aahing at their soupy eyes and Oreo fur. And then I saw something that made me stop scrolling.

One of the puppies was named Brutus.

I emailed an application. It felt questionable. It was too soon. I judged myself for doing it. But it felt like the universe was telling me something. That Brutus was telling me something.

I never heard back from the woman who headed the rescue in Utah. But it gave me what I really needed. Permission to seriously think about adopting a dog. I like to believe it was Brutus who encouraged me on, who found another way to comfort me through grief.

I was aware that it was a rapid 180. To go from swearing off dog companionship for life—to looking to adopt another dog within a month of losing Brutus. But it was the beginning of the pandemic, when we were Zooming with our next-door neighbors and only leaving our houses to pick up curbside groceries. The house was painfully quiet without Brutus scampering around, and I had more free time than I knew what to do with. And that free time was full of the searing grief of losing my mom. It had only been two months since her funeral. The idea of getting a puppy was logistically possible, in a way that it normally wouldn't feel. We were working remotely and traveling nowhere.

A week or so later, I saw a litter in Eugene with heeler-mix puppies and started flipping through the photos of each one. I'd added heelers to my PetFinder rotation. I wouldn't have known to even look for heelers, if not for the litter in Utah with little Brutus.

There was a puppy with reddish fur, scooped up in the arms of his foster, with his paws hooked over the edge of her elbow. His tail was unnaturally long, dangling down to the floor like a jungle cat's. His eyes were rimmed with thick black lines like tattooed eyeliner. His ears folded and flopped in little triangles. He looked like he wanted to jump down and find a sock to chew up, but first, he wanted some snuggles.

He looked equal parts mischievous and loving. A cuddly rascal. He looked like he would grow into a dog that could run through the mountains all day and then snuggle in a tent all night. He would chase as many sticks as you would throw him and never run out of kisses. His name was Rocky, but I knew I'd change it. I immediately submitted an application.

I got a call from the rescue a few hours later. I was fifth in line for the litter. It was the early days of the pandemic, when adopting a pet could be a cutthroat affair. On Saturday, I would get ten minutes to meet whatever puppies were left after four other families had their pick.

All I could think about was how likely it was that Rocky would be gone by the time I got there. I did absolutely nothing to prepare for having a puppy in the house because I was so certain Rocky would get adopted before I even had the chance to meet him.

When we walked into the rescue on Saturday morning, my heart was pounding. Four weeks ago, I didn't think I wanted another dog, and now, I was convinced that my dog was in this litter. And I was certain Rocky would be the first to go.

The clock ticked 10:40, and it was our turn to go in to where the puppies were kept. I watched a woman walk out holding Bandit, the gray puppy with a dark burglar's mask over his eyes. I exhaled a sigh of relief that it wasn't my little red rascal. My pulse raced as we entered.

I turned the corner and looked into the puppy dome that was set up with the four remaining dogs. I stared into the pile of puppies and my heart jumped. Rocky was still there.

I squealed. And then I walked over and scooped him up. He immediately melted into my arms. I felt his little puppy heart beating wildly. I buried my nose into his soft puppy fur and kissed him.

"He's our puppy," I breathed to Ian. The puppy-formerly-known-as-Rocky melted deeper into my body and nuzzled his nose into my chest.

We brought him home and Rocky became Dilly. And Dilly immediately filled our house with love and joy and silly puppy play. I'll never know how it's possible that you can look at a puppy's picture and be certain he's meant to be your best friend. But I knew Dilly was my dog. And Dilly was exactly the snuggly rascal I knew he would be.

I was still deep in grief, but he reminded me that the biggest love and warmest joy can live alongside the darkest grief.

Dilly made it easy to feel love amid grief. There were days when I don't know if I would have cracked a smile or felt warmth without Dilly.

Every day, I'd look at him and feel that he already had my whole heart. I'd stroke his soft puppy fur and know he was going to shatter my heart someday. And every day, I'd look at him and know a life with him would be worth the pain.

Mile 450,
Columbia River Gorge

I'm picking my way down a steep hillside when it hits me. Every fiber of my being wants my mom. The urge to call her crashes into me like a tidal wave. The realization I can't is a sneakier wave that pulls me under water, flailing and gasping for air.

My mom was always my first call. Through every high and low. And while I'm running through the highest highs and the lowest lows, all I want is to talk to her.

The closer I get to the bridge, the more I long for my mother. There is nothing I want more on this earth than to share this moment with her. To tell her I'm going to do it. To tell her I'm going to do it for her. The yearning for her is alive with me on the trail, dragging me into the dark belly of the crater she left behind.

Tall ferns rise up around the trail. The last rays of sunlight spill through the trees and dance across the leafy tendrils of the ferns. I search for her in the soft beams of light. Grasping to hold onto any piece of her I can find.

I turn my gaze inward. I let myself fall deeper into the longing for my mom. When I decided to do this run, there was part of me that wondered if I was trying to outrun grief, if this run was an escape route from my pain, but in this moment, I know it has only given me a place to feel every ridge of it. It's been a way to move forward, but I haven't left my grief behind; it is right here with me.

Night descends over the Gorge. I grab my headlamp from my pack. I'll finish this run in the dark.

1971
Bristol, Vermont

My mother lost her mom to ovarian cancer when she was just nineteen. It was something I always knew about her. But it was a fact of her life before me that I didn't attach enough emotion to. Like what hospital she was born in and where she went to school. I didn't understand what it really meant to have lost her mom so young. How devastating it must have been for her. How she must have felt her entire world cave in on her and strand her in darkness.

I didn't understand it until she got sick and I had to think about losing her. At thirty-five, I felt too young to be motherless. I couldn't imagine being nineteen and losing my mom. She was just a child.

"I remember going to the funeral," my dad told me. They grew up in the same small town and her mom was one of his elementary school-teachers. "When they walked in with the casket, Andrea was draped over the edge, wailing for her mom."

I didn't used to understand what my mom endured, but I feel like that wail lives inside me now.

Her father died just two years later, and she was parentless before she graduated college.

Now that I know this loss for myself, I see my mother differently. Now that I live with the vibrations of that wail inside of me, I am in disbelief of the woman she became through that heartbreak.

I'd always been amazed by my mom and her wholehearted way of living. But knowing she chased that life after having her heart shattered by loss was stunning.

It helped me feel hope. To believe I could live through the worst pain I'd ever known and still live a beautiful life, just like my mom.

Mile 458,
Columbia River Gorge

I see a glimmer of light through the black night. I run toward it. A moth to a flame.

It's Ian and Gabriel, with Dilly in tow, eyes glowing. Dilly bounds up to me when he sees me, his long Wiffle bat tail wagging wildly in every direction. My heart bursts at the sight of him. He showers me in enthusiastic puppy kisses. Here he is again, making it impossible not to feel love and joy when I'm immersed in pain and darkness. Reminding me that I can hold all of those feelings in my heart, at the same time.

I see another flicker of light through the black night. Headlamps glow like fireflies. My heart jumps again when I realize it's more friends who have waited for hours through the night, watching for the beam of my headlamp, to cheer me into the finish. I will finish this run surrounded by the same love and support that has carried me through grief. That has carried me from one side of Oregon to the other.

I run toward their light.

Everything hurts with every step. I feel how I have emptied myself to get here. How I have asked myself to dig deeper than I ever thought I could—and to keep going. This run has stripped me down to my most vulnerable and rawest self.

But I'm not weak in this state. I'm steps away from running the Oregon PCT faster than any other runner before me. I'm a million steps into the most powerful, special, and courageous run of my life. I am running and living like my mom always did.

Soon it's another cluster of headlamps. Glistening like stars below.

I run toward them, letting the light reel me through each step. The night sky burns with stars overhead.

I see the shadows of the bridge looming before me. I am almost close enough to touch it.

I imagine reaching my hand out and pressing it into the cold metal of the sign that marks the northern border of Oregon. I feel everything as I think about reaching the other side of Oregon and finishing this run. The exhaustion. The ecstasy. The love. The longing. The joy. The grief.

I feel that this is why I ran across Oregon. This was what I needed after losing my mother. To move through the wreckage of grief and feel everything that can exist alongside the rubble, and what can shine through it. To realize there's so much in life we can't control, but there are choices that are ours to make.

The loss of my mother thrust me into unbearable pain and asked me to decide how to live after feeling the deepest cuts of grief.

I have felt the slippery temptation of trying to shield myself from more pain, of locking myself in a bunker to protect myself from heartbreak, of living a muted existence and choosing safety over vulnerability.

But I feel how deciding to do this run was the first step in making a different choice. When I started this run, I reignited a smoldering fire, and embraced all of the fear and uncertainty that burns with it. I feel how following in my mother's footsteps led me to a place where I'm willing to risk more heartbreak and pain for the chance to know a wholehearted life and the brightest love. A place where I can see vulnerability as a gateway, instead of a threat. Just like she did after enduring her own worst pain.

I know my mom would never choose to lose her mom when she did. And I know she lived a different life because she did. I feel, in this moment, how both things can be true.

I run onto the bridge leading a train of headlamps. Light beams in every direction, cutting through the darkness. An orchestra of cheers swells around me as I take my final steps across the grated metal.

I touch the bridge beneath the sign that marks the Oregon border and it unleashes the mess of emotions I knew it would. As I stop running, my legs buckle beneath me. I gave this trail everything I had. And it gave me so much in return.

Ian folds me into a hug and Dilly leaps up to give me more kisses. My friends are jumping and screaming all around me.

I look down at my watch. I finished my run across Oregon in 7 days, 19 hours, and 23 minutes, a new overall record on the trail.

I made it all the way to the other side of Oregon, but I know this run isn't the end of anything. I'll keep going, carrying my grief and love together, with my heart open.

EPILOGUE

I'm trying to put on my Chacos when my brother calls. It's just three days after I reached the Bridge of the Gods and my feet are still swollen and covered in blisters. They butt up against the straps of my sandals and refuse to go a breath further.

I answer the phone, my voice still strained with fatigue, my throat still scratchy with trail dust.

"Hi, Jameson."

I hear my brother crying on the other end of the line. He fights to get his words out. I hold my breath, my heart hammers. I know he's about to deliver the worst possible news about Jess.

"Jess is getting moved to hospice," he says. "They think she only has days left."

"Oh, Jameson," I sigh. I start crying, and we stay on the phone together, neither of us able to say anything for several minutes.

"I'll book a flight right away," I tell him. My insides crumble.

I don't know if I'm physically capable of walking through an airport terminal, or of putting on shoes to travel, but I know I need to get on a plane and fly to Vermont as soon as I can.

I shuffle upstairs to start looking for flights. My heart aches for my brother—and for Jess. It hasn't even been seven months since we buried our mom. It feels like it should be against the rules of the universe for my brother to lose his wife while the wounds from our mother's death are still burning red.

But, of course, that's not how life works. There's no logic to explain this. And no sense to be made of Jess's death. It's just heart-wrenching. An unimaginable tragedy becoming a cruel reality.

I think back to their wedding, the last day we all had together before the dominoes started to fall.

I remember how emotional I got watching my brother and feeling how much love radiated between him and Jess, and from the hundreds of guests to them. The love was palpable, like you could reach into the air and hold onto its warmth.

It was the most beautiful thing, to see my little brother surrounded by so much love, and to see him so happy, because he'd found such bright love with Jess.

I booked a flight and walked over to the closet to start packing in a stunned trance. Each step to get ready to board a plane to Vermont felt entirely too familiar and haunting.

I knew I couldn't fully understand what my brother was feeling, as he hung up the phone and walked back to Jess's bedside to hold her hand. But I knew the heartache he was feeling was tethered to the immense love I'd seen and felt and loved between him and Jess.

I knew that same love would thrust him into the deepest canyon of grief. And I knew I couldn't make anything better for him. All I could do was flick on my headlamp and stand in the dark, shining light and love toward him while he moved through the worst heartbreak, reminding him that the same world that thrusts us into the darkest pain is also swimming with the most powerful love, and maybe that's why we keep going, when it feels like we can't take another step.

APPENDICES

WHAT IT TAKES
TO RUN 60 MILES A DAY

I ran for at least 16–17 hours a day. I was usually on the trail before 6:00 A.M. and ran well past sunset.

- I needed to eat at least 100–200 calories an hour and substantial food at the end of the day.
- I slept for 4–5 hours a night for recovery, sometimes a bit less if the running took longer.

I received support through crewing, where friends met me with food, gear, and water along the trail. They could help me address issues like blisters and chafing. I was also paced by friends, where they'd run anywhere from 3 to 60 miles with me, to keep me company and keep me moving. The only limitation for a supported FKT is that you power your own body through every mile.

THE THINGS I CARRIED

I wore a hydration pack throughout the run that was stuffed with spare gear and running essentials. Some of my go-to items included:

- Food—I eat more real food than sports nutrition when running because it works better for me. I carried things like candy, chips, peanut butter pretzels, Oreos, and baked goods. And I ate more substantial food at crew stops, including mashed potatoes, ramen, burritos, and Coke.
- A Garmin inReach—a satellite device that tracked my run and allowed me to send and receive messages from my crew while outside of cell service.
- A headlamp and spare batteries.
- Small but mighty essentials like sunscreen, ChapStick, anti-chafe lubricant, first aid supplies, and foot care.
- Extra layers, including a water- and wind-resistant jacket.
- Water. I always had at least a 1.5-liter bladder on me.

A NOTE ON MILEAGE
FROM THE AUTHOR

As most runners know, various maps, watches, and apps will report different mileage data. The chapter headers in this book are based on what my GPS watch tracked for mileage during the run. And the narrative is based on the mileage I mapped out when planning the run, primarily using Gaia GPS and the National Geographic maps for the Pacific Crest Trail. There are some small discrepancies between the two numbers throughout the story.

ACKNOWLEDGMENTS

There is nothing about this book that I could have done without incredible and generous support. The run. The grief. The writing. I was surrounded and buoyed by loving, kind, amazing humans through all of it. There are no words to adequately express how grateful I am for every person who sat with me through grief, joined me for the run across Oregon, and helped me write a whole dang book, but I'll try to write a few to capture a small sliver of my gratitude.

Let's start with the run. When people ask whether I went for a supported or self-supported FKT, I like to say I went for the extra-supported version. I was spoiled with support for my run across Oregon, and while it was unquestionably the hardest run of my life, it was also the best.

Thank you to the friends who crewed and paced me from one side of the state to the other, and shared miles, snacks, and trailside dance parties along the way: Ian Petersen; Danielle Snyder; Eli Tome; Nicole Antoinette; Tom Grossmith; Jameson Clover; Alli Hartz; Amy and Caleb Holt; Eric, Gretchen, and Fitz Roy Suchman; Emily Spognardi; Sarah Conklin; Lauren Sommers; Stacy Levichev; Nick Cady; Gabriel Hoy; Gordon Freeman; Lucy Barton; David Miller; and Julian Smith. Thank you for bringing the fun and the flair, surprising me with your beautiful selves and trail magic, running with me through most every condition and emotion, and belting out Taylor Swift and Celine Dion songs in the middle of the woods. I had the time of my life running across Oregon with all of you.

Ian, thank you for crewing me through every single minute of the run and working as hard as I did to make the run a success. Danielle, thank you for showing me that camaraderie and competitiveness can coexist, and that we are our best selves and runners when we lift each other up.

And thank you to the Hunt and family, who made sure Charlton Lake was one heck of a party. And to the Hunters who couldn't make it, but were an integral part of my introduction to trail running: Evan St. Cyr, Dan Olmstead, Daniel and Ashley Force, Justin and Kim Russell, Andrew Sheridan, Gracie Lynne, Callie Cooper, Christian Beck, Lewis Taylor, Tom Atkins, Jon Meyers, and Joe Uhan, who also provided invaluable physical therapy during the run. Thank you for all of the chips, beers, and Tuesdays.

Thank you to the 918 generous people who supported my run through donations to the Brave Like Gabe Foundation. You helped me raise $34,343 to support rare cancer research and to create more treatment options for people like my mom and Gabe Grunewald. You all gave me so much hope and purpose during this run. And thank you to Rachel Bearbower, for sharing her fundraising skills and pushing me to aim higher. And thank you to everyone who cheered me on from afar, I felt it.

And now for the book, which might have been an even harder undertaking than the run. Thank you to the friends who shared writing dates, pep talks, and marionberry blueberry pastry vessels, especially Emma Stockman, Nicole Antoinette, Sarah Conklin, and Margaret Martin. And to Emma Stockman and Margaret Martin, who read and workshopped chapters along the way and helped me make this a stronger and more vulnerable book, I appreciate you and your brilliant and thoughtful feedback so much. And thank you to Ali Feller, Jameson Halnon, and Lauren Sommers, who read the full book in my final stretch of writing and convinced me not to burn the whole thing while I was battling my greatest insecurities.

This book wouldn't have gone anywhere without my incredible agent Stephany Evans, who was the best champion for this story. Stephany also got into running later in life and immediately connected with my mom and understood why many more people should read about Andrea Halnon. Stephany has her own impressive resume of running accomplishments and I've loved working with someone who gets me, and my mom, like Stephany does. And a huge thank you to the entire team at Pegasus Books, especially my editor Jessica Case, for believing in this story and turning it into a real, live book. Thank you for your thoughtful, enthusiastic, and patient guidance. Thank you, Ian Petersen, for creating the maps throughout this book. And thank you to Lane County Arts Council for supporting my art.

I don't know where to begin with thanking the people who got me through grief—and continue to get me through grief. To everyone who has showed up with love, hugs, food, texts, dogs, calls, and company, thank you for holding me through the worst days of loss. Grief is a bear. And I couldn't have moved forward without your love and help. And a huge thank you to Ellie Klopp, who's helped me get through many emotional challenges, including my mother's cancer and death, and who gave me a safe space to revisit my rawest grief while writing this book.

And endless hugs and thank yous to my mother's closest friends and family, and my dad, Steve, who showed up for her in so many big and small ways. It gave me so much comfort to see how loved and supported she was by all of you.

Thank you to my brother, Jameson Halnon, who's gone through more than makes sense in his own life, but still finds enough space to support me through everything I do. Our mom was always our biggest cheerleader and Jameson has stepped up to try and fill her shoes as the greatest hype sibling. I hit the brother jackpot with Jameson and I'm so grateful he is my family.

And Ian, thank you for sticking with me and supporting me through the lowest lows, in grief, running, and writing, and for sharing so many highs. I'm so lucky to have you in my life. And to my Dilly Pickle Chip, thank you for making sure I always feel love, no matter how distraught

I may be. And Brutus, thank you for showing me what all of the fuss is about with dogs.

And thank you to my mom, Andrea, who not only made me a runner, but also a reader and a lover of the written word. It breaks my heart that she can't read this, but it's easy to imagine how excited she would be to see and read her daughter's book. She probably would have broken the internet posting about it.

It is a gift to share her with all of *you* through these pages. Thank you for reading.